I HEALED ON PURPOSE

Detoxing the Wounded Soul

Athena Jackson

I Prevail Coaching

Published by Athena Jackson

ISBN: 9781794045347

Athena Jackson

All right reserved, this book is protected to the copyright laws of the United States of America. This book may not be copied for commercial gain or profit.

They are not intended in any way to be or imply an endorsement by Athena Jackson

Cover design: Javonte Pitts

Cover Photography: Canva

Interior Design: Athena Jackson

Printed in the United States of America

Athena Jackson

Contents

Acknowledgments 5
Preface: My Healing Journey 9
Damaged Emotions 13
    Emotional Detoxing 18
The Wounded Soul 21
The Wound of Rejection 31
The Wound of Abandonment 40
The Wound of Humiliation 65
The Wound of Injustice 64
The Wounds of Betrayal 71
Soul Cleanse Days 1-14 77
Spiritual Boot Camp Days 1-6 201

Acknowledgments

I want to dedicate "I Healed on Purpose – Detoxing the Wounded Soul" to my Pastors Mary Ellen and Charles Crutcher, who both have inspired, challenged, and empowered me to release my inner giant by facing my fears and embracing my authentic self. I love you both to life. To my Kingdom Life Church family, friends, and loved ones who believe in and support, me thank you.

Thanks to my clients, who have enrolled in my "Heal on Purpose" Coaching program, and the women in my "Heal on purpose" Sip and Chat support group, thank you for your willingness to be transparent. You ladies keep me motivated to keep writing, researching and teaching people to heal their soul wounds.

Athena Jackson

To my amazing husband, Morris Jackson, who continues to offer this love and support, I appreciate and love you so much. To my children Brenda, Renee, Linell, Lionel, Diamond, Donavon, and Pamela, you all are my reason; I love you all dearly. To my mother, Brenda Woodford, who prays, counsels, and supports me in my endeavors; words can't express my gratitude. Thanks for believing in me. I love you!

Furthermore, to Tameko Martin and I Prevail Coaching staff, thank you for helping me birth my vision for "I Healed on Purpose." To everyone who reads this book, may this book bless you and help you heal the wounds of your soul.

CONGRATULATIONS! By purchasing "I Healed on Purpose," you have decided to take your power back and heal the wounds of your past. The healing process can be a bit scary because emotional detoxing can be painful, and yes, it takes work. Emotional healing requires having the courage to address and make peace with your history. I applaud you for being bold enough to stare fear in the face and fight for your right to be authentic.

You must embrace your healing process. Healing doesn't happen automatically; you have to intentional about your emotional health. Embracing the process means taking reasonability for who you are and where you are now emotionally. Your financial, educational, and social status has nothing to do with your emotional health. You can be successful in these areas and very well be emotionally unhealthy. As a matter of fact, some people use these statuses to mask their wounds. The church is another place where people go to mask their emotional wounds. To heal these wounds, you must be willing to lose the mask and expose your fears so they can be free. You didn't get here overnight, and you won't heal overnight. If you stay the course and apply the principles outlined in this book, you will find that this healing journey gets more comfortable with time.

Athena Jackson

    I am proud of you, and I believe the heavenly angels are smiling as you have canceled the enemy's assignment in your life by choosing to heal. You will see doors began to open as you gain the confidence to knock on them. In the days to come, I am going to provide you with information to identify and destroy old unhealthy, and toxic emotions that keep you stuck. You will adopt a belief system that unleashes your inner champion.

Get ready to release your emotional baggage and heal, on purpose.

PREFACE:

MY HEALING JOURNEY

For many years wore mask, trying to hide my emotional pain. The thought of dealing with my painful, traumatic events was unbearable and overwhelming; I chose to suppress my emotions and pretend I was ok. I experienced a considerable amount of trauma in my childhood: sexual abuse, physical abuse, humiliation, abandonment, and rejection. I was scared to face my past, and I feared I would be vulnerable and labeled. I can't begin to count the nights I laid awake silently screaming to be set free from the emotional pain that governed my mind. Pride would not allow me to move forward, so I stayed in the mental bondage that my fears created.

I was born with a heart condition Mitro Valve Prolapse and a murmur. The stress that the trauma caused in my childhood added weight on my heart. I developed arthritis, high blood pressure, experienced heart failure, pulmonary hypertension, I had a mild stroke, and hyperthyroidism. Most of these issues were a result of my unresolved emotional issues.

My damaged emotions caused me to become co-dependent in my relationships; I ended up in some pretty dysfunctional, even narcissistic relationships. I was suffering emotionally, physically, mentally, and spiritually. I spent many sleepless nights with silent uncontrollable tears, as I reflected on the events from the past. For years I hid my pain in shame. The wounds of humiliation, rejection, and abandonment held me captive to a limiting belief system of not being enough. I didn't realize that I was a conqueror, a strong woman, or a soldier; instead, I felt defeated. Although I made contributions to other people's happiness, I had no clue on what to do to quiet the inner pain that taunted me day and night. Crazy right! It wasn't until I stared death in the face, that I realized I had not even begun to live. After recovery from surgery, I decided at that point that if God allowed me a new opportunity, I would lay aside my pride and do what I need to do to heal.

My healing journey began in a hospital bed at Mt. Carmel Hospital, hours after I woke up from surgery and was able to grasp my thoughts. I made up my mind that I would no longer allow my fears created from soul wounds, to control my decisions.

I chose to take off the mask and get naked before God so he could heal my wounded soul. I took responsibility for my issues and intentionally decided to heal emotionally.

Healing on purpose meant that I would have to acknowledge the pain from my past traumatic experiences. I was challenged to recognize the emotional pain from which I was running. I read books, attended workshops, conferences, attended counseling, and developed a close relationship with my creator. I needed all these tools and resources to be successful on my journey to be free from my previous years of trauma. Not only did I suffer as a child, but I continued to suffer as an adult.

I made decisions in my adulthood from my toxic emotions that created more chains to my emotional prison of shame and guilt. I operated out of an "I am not enough" mindset.

As I began to develop a closer relationship with my creator and embrace his purpose for my life, I gained the courage to heal the wounds from my past. I realized that I had it all wrong, I wasn't worthless, or damaged goods, or less than, instead, I am a strong woman, a conqueror a soldier, who beat the odds. I am enough.

Athena Jackson

I now walk boldly in my purpose. My faith is unwavering, and I embrace the fact that I am fearful and wonderfully made. I am destined to soar.

If you desire to live a fulfilling, rewarding life, you must make peace with the pain of your past and heal your soul wounds. Running from your past will create a stockpile of emotional issues. Consider adopting a lifestyle that allows you to deal with the daggers that life throws at you. Each time I experienced emotional pain, I revisit the steps that are laid out in the proceeding pages.

My goal is that every person that reads this book experiences the freedom that emotional healing offers. In this journey of life, we are sure to experience some trauma, whether it be the loss of a loved one, break ups, betrayal, abuse, any event that causes us pain, but it's how we deal with those events that make the difference. This book, *"I Healed on Purpose,"* is designed to help you detox your wounded soul. It will help you destroy unproductive beliefs that hold your inner champion hostage.

"I Healed On Purpose," will allow you to make peace with your past, and it will also aid you in dealing with future painful events you may face.

Chapter 1

DAMAGED EMOTIONS

Definition of Emotion

e·mo·tion

əˈmōSH(ə)n/

noun

plural noun: **emotions**

1. A natural instinctive state of mind deriving from one's circumstances, mood, or relationships with others.

2. Instinctive or intuitive feeling as distinguished from reasoning or knowledge.

   Our experiences create our emotions. Life offers an array of emotional skills such as love, hate, trust, anger, happiness, sadness, excitement, bitterness, and resentment, along with other emotions. These emotions can also influence our decisions. For example, if you are a victim of domestic violence, you may not be open to dating in fear of being hurt. You may also jump from relationship to relationship looking for validation. Your past painful relationships lay the groundwork that influences the fear and distrust in future relationships. You may settle for less than you deserve because of your feelings of unworthiness and low self-esteem. All these feelings were created from past experiences and caused you to be emotionally damaged.

Damaged emotions are the perceptions and feelings derived out of negative actions, words, and attitudes that were afflicted on us, whether it was a single or ongoing event. Most damaged emotions are often a result of our childhood. Some causes of damaged emotions come from the following:

- **Grief** - A divorce or loss of a loved one.

- **Parental indifference** - actions that produce a sense of unworthiness.
- **Physical/Sexual abuse** - painful memories that haunt the emotions & cripple life.
- **Rejection /Abandonment** - a sense of being unwanted and unloved.
- People bury their emotions for various reasons. Some have been so traumatized

that they have difficulty recalling their traumatic events while others pretend it never happened. Some people choose to adopt a victim mentality.

- They use their emotional wounds as an excuse to stay in their comfort zones.
- Some people won't deal with their past issues because the pain is overwhelming.
- People also escape from pain by overachieving and becoming self-indulged. There is nothing wrong with advancing, but the problems start when you use it to escape reality.

People hop in and out of relationships running from emotional pain. They are looking for love and ways to numb their discomfort rather than take time to deal with their broken hearts. Some eventually become addicts, turning to drugs, alcohol, food, and sex for temporary comfort, which as a result, creates more emotional pain.

Some symptoms from damaged emotions;

- **Low Self-Esteem** - Feelings of inadequacy, worthless, or inferiority.
- **Fear of Failure** - is when we allow **fear** to stop us from doing the things

that can move us forward to achieve our goals.

- **Fear of Rejection** - fear that people won't accept you due to who you are.

- **Co-dependency** - Overcompensating to be accepted and basing your choices on your need to be liked and the opinions of other people.

- **Dysfunctional Relationships** - The inability to relate and respond to others in an inappropriate in a productive manner.

- **Defeated Mentality** - People who have great intentions but continue to self-sabotage with the cycle of resolve, defeat, confession, and rededication. The cycle goes on.

- **Pretenders** - people who have learned the art of acting as if their life is perfect and parade around like the trauma never happened.

- **Controlling** – anxiety-driven, become angry, and feeling betrayed when people don't do what you want, lack of trust, and having a history of combative relationships.

People get stuck and allow their painful experiences to rob them of true happiness. "*I Healed On Purpose*" offers you the opportunity to honor your pain, grieve, confront issues, make peace with it, and find your authentic voice. Choosing to heal your wounded soul will change your life forever.

Chapter 2

EMOTIONAL DETOXING

A person's perception usually conditions their emotions, which in turn has a predominant influence in their decision-making (the will). A healthy emotional state is necessary to make good decisions, e.g., strategic decisions in a moment of anger. Generally, one should make decisions on principle, and not so much in their emotions. To alter the feelings and your will, you must change the way your belief system. To change your belief system, you must dislodge and interrupt inaccurate thought patterns by replacing them with the new information daily. You must replace these thought patterns formed by our emotions and perceptions with truth which is he word of God, and positive resources.

Just as your body needs to detox and rid of toxins that keep you from achieving optimal health. Damaged emotions can contribute to an unhealthy lifestyle. "*I Healed on Purpose*" Detoxing the Wounded Soul, offers you the opportunity to detox your wounded soul and transform your mind. Your toxic emotions have wreaked havoc on your mind and body long enough. No longer will you make decisions from a limited belief system, sabotage your dreams, harbor feelings of shame, guilt, anger, resentment, and bitterness.

To heal your wounded soul, you must acknowledge the traumatic event(s) and the role they played in forming these wounds. *"I Healed on Purpose"* will help you identify which of the five emotional wounds of which you are operating. These five wounds are rejection, humiliation, abandonment, injustice, and betrayal.

You will learn how negative emotions such as anger, sadness, frustration, fear, anxiety, jealousy, low self-esteem, hold you captive to your past, and how to deal with them. You will have the opportunity to complete self-assessments that will aid you in your detox and healing process. Emotional detoxing can be painful, so I recommend when you get that section, you read and complete these steps one day at a time. Allow yourself time to heal. Working ahead can be overwhelming and can result in you abandoning the process. If you miss a day, pick up where you left off. It may help to set a few reminders on your phone to remind you to read this book at the same time every day. The time has come to live your best life, and it all starts here and now. The great news is that this

Athena Jackson

book is going to empower you to experience the mental freedom to be your authentic self.

Chapter 3

THE WOUNDED SOUL

Our soul is made up of three parts, our mind, our will, and our emotions.

Our Mind

Proverbs 2:10 "Wisdom will enter your heart, / And knowledge will be pleasant to your soul."

Lamentations 3:20 "My soul remembers them well," this indicates that the soul can remember things.

Our Will

Job 7:15 - "My soul would choose," and 6:7 says, "My soul refuses." To choose and to refuse are both decisions and functions of the will.

Chronicles 22:19 - "Now set your heart and your soul to seek after Jehovah your God."

Our Emotions

Psalm 42:1 - As the deer pants for streams of water, so my soul pants for you, my God.

Job 30:25 - Have I not wept for those in trouble?   Has not my soul grieved for the poor?

Athena Jackson

A soul wound is emotional pain or a negative belief that a part of you takes on as a result of an adverse or traumatic event such as shame, abandonment, humiliation, betrayal, or rejection. This wound causes you to take on a false identity and see life through the filters of the wounds of your soul.

Changing your belief systems is the key to healing your wounded soul. Getting to the core of why you reason the way you do is a crucial step in ridding your soul of negative emotions. Soul wounds are made up of bitterness, unforgiveness, shame, guilt, resentment, and anger. These emotions are the breeding ground for sickness and disease. You are what you allow to lie in your soul. Illness and disease breed in the wounded soul, so it is vital to detox and heal so your soul becomes healthy. As you become closer to your creator and allow your thoughts to line up with his word, you will shift your way of thinking.

The bible says in 3rd John 2:2, "Beloved, I wish above all things that thou mayest prosper and be in health, even as thy soul prospereth." God's will is for you to be free from the fears of your wounded emotions.

A wounded soul will sabotage every area of your life. It invites in demonic spirits to have the authority to attack your mind, body, as well as destroy relationships, including your relationship with God.

Ephesians 6:12 "For we wrestle not against flesh and blood, but against principalities, against powers, against the rulers of the darkness of this world, against spiritual wickedness in high places."

How your soul gets wounded

Your soul becomes wounded when there is a point of trauma. Your traumatic experience creates a system of thoughts and cycles of behavior. For example, the trauma of rejection releases into the emotional or mental heart of a child abandoned by a parent. The incident creates a negative emotional wound that is often reinforced by other events.

Over time the injured soul creates a stronghold of fear and rejection that further creates contaminated imaginations, false expectations, and unrealistic demands. As the wounded soul lashes out against people, relational misfires occur that create even more rejection and wounds. Emotional walls begin to build, and the pattern of unhealthy relationships are established.

The Major Causes of Most Wounds

- Physical, mental, verbal - abuse.
- Sexual abuse - Familiar figure touching you in ways that are not right.
- Abandonment - Through Death, Separation, Divorce, Addiction or being bullied (in your childhood or as an adult.)
- Rejection by relatives and friends.
- Major disappointments and broken promises I thought I could count on them or trust them.
- Divorce and separation- Everyone gets infected.
- Major moral failure - adultery, abortion, abandonment.

Soul wounds robs your time

The Greek word for "heart" in this passage is *Cardia*. Our heart is the emotional center of our being and the capacity of moral preference. It is the part of us that produces desire and makes us tick. It is the core of our minds, where we make our decisions and defines who we are.

The adversary sets out to attack our hearts, the inner mind we each have, and contaminate it with wounds. Many times, the enemy will use an old, unrecognized, and unresolved emotional wound as a gateway to attack you. It is possible to experience hurt and bitterness about something going on in your life right now that stings because of an old and unresolved soul wound.

It is vital to your prophetic destiny that you heal your wounded soul. Soul wounds will drag you down a path of continued defeat.

Athena Jackson

Your life moves in the opposite direction of your purpose, and your inner emotional turmoil ultimately manifests in dramatic outer behavior.

As our core wounds deepen, we begin to put up barriers of protection to keep other people from hurting us. These barriers eventually cause us to become trapped within ourselves. Soul wounds rob your time, this is the reason the enemy attacks us in our childhood or early adulthood he knows the younger he can distort ones belief system, the stronger the hold he has on their mind.

When you decide to heal on purpose, you are making a conscious choice to overcome the strongholds of your mind. These strongholds must be dealt with so that the power of God can cleanse your soul through the resurrection power blood of Jesus Christ.

Studying soul wounds lead me to the realization that my physical sickness was a direct result of being bitter, resentful, and unforgiveness, each of these formed from emotional wounds. Arthritis, heart disease, thyroid issues, were all indications that my soul was wounded. I was bound to sickness by the scars of my soul.

As I learned to overcome the fears from my soul wounds, healing began to manifest. I was free from the mental bondage, and I began to live my life on purpose. The wounded soul can cause sickness and disease and can ultimately send you to an early grave, causing us to forfeit God's perfect plan for us.

Once you are aware of your core soul wound and how it affects your belief system, you can begin to apply the principals in this book. Your life will drastically change.

"I Healed on Purpose" will help you identify:

- What is your core wound?

- How has it shaped your belief system?

- What fear and limitations have your wounds caused you?

- Who your creator is and why it is vital to your healing process that you develop a close relationship with him?

- Who am I?

Athena Jackson

- What is my purpose?

- Why is it important that I allow my inner champion to be released?

Fears Formed from Soul Wounds

Unattended wounds create fears that eventually choose your lifestyle. Fears causes people to live in a false reality. Take the fear of rejection, for instance. This fear creates a false reality of not being good enough. This false reality will make you abandon your purpose. The confidence you need to succeed is lost in your need to be accepted and to please others. Your desire to be validated will make you ask for approval to shine. The problem in seeking permission to shine is that most people don't want you to outshine them so that they won't permit you. This is why you must identify your emotional wounds so that you can overcome the fears and limiting belief systems that are associated with those wounds. God created the sun to shine and every morning without permission, the suns does exactly it was created to do.

It doesn't compare itself to the moon or the stars or any other light, it simply shines. God wants you to shine just as he created you to without begging for anyone else approval.

The next few chapters will cover five different childhood wounds — rejection, abandonment, humiliation, injustice, and betrayal. Identify your core wound and the other wounds that accompany it, so you will focus on healing from them.

As you identify your core wounds will learn:
- Why you reason the way you do.
- How your traumatic experiences shaped your limiting belief system.
- How to heal your soul wounds

Chapter 4

THE WOUND OF REJECTION

The enemy uses rejection to make us feel valueless and worthless. Denial is one of Satan's most effective forms of oppression. He uses rejection as a weapon to keep us separated from God, and from walking in our purpose. I often refer to the rejection wound as the foundational would of the other four wounds (abandonment, humiliation, injustice, and betrayal. These wounds are formed from the wounds of rejection. Rejection undermines and prevents harmonious relationships. It is one of the most untreated illness and because if the wound of rejection people suffers from depression and anxiety. People become bitter, angry and unforgiving. Rejection causes people to become paralyzed with the fear of not being enough.

Co-dependency and the inability to completely accept and love yourself for whom you stem from is the root of rejection. Rejection affects the very core of who you are and plays a significant role in shaping your belief system. People who have unaddressed trauma and abuse, suffer from the root of rejection and the toxic thought patterns that accompany them. The origin of rejection

Athena Jackson

produces the fruit of rejection such as (Place a checkmark by the ones you can identify with)

- Fabricated personalities (being somebody you aren't, to be accepted)
- Rejection others to avoid rejection.
- The need to fit in and be accepted.
- Self-pity where a person feels bad for themselves being all alone.
- Inability to receive constructive criticism.
- Rejection creates an environment of starvation for love, or you just don't fit in.

- Blaming God for everything
- Feeling unworthy and hopeless
- Rebellion
- Insecure
- The need to be right about everything
- The need to be needed
- Fear of failure
- Envy, jealousy, and even hate can be rooted in rejection
- Fear of confrontation (because your identity is based upon what they think of you)

The root of rejection causes you to base your identity on how your parents or other people treat you. The root of rejection is the belief system that forms as a result of the traumatic event(s) you experienced and your perception from those experiences. The closer the person is who wounded you, the deeper the root of rejection.

As a child, I internalized my father's absence to mean I wasn't good enough and that I was second best. This false reality causes me to feel unworthy and compromise my standards to be accepted.

Overcoming the root of rejection requires you to embrace and accept God's love for you. He isn't angry with you and God is not punishing you. You must understand that God is not the blame for the people who hurt and took advantage of you. God

Athena Jackson

gave man free will, and man chose to disobey and reject his instruction him sin entered this world. Rejection and shame were born out of sin. Look how Cain killed his brother Able, although Able did no wrong to him, he was jealous (rejection) of Able. The same goes for the person who hurt you. You may have done nothing to deserve their actions, but they acted wrongly, most likely from their wounded soul.

God desires you to be whole and healed from your damaged emotions. He wants your belief system to line up with his word.

Psalms 139:14 says, "I praise you because I am fearfully and wonderfully made; your works are wonderful; I know that full well." The bible also says, "We are uniquely created in the image of God. We are set apart from all other creation. St. John: 16 says, "For God so loved the world that he gave his only begotten son, that whosoever believeth in him shall not perish but have everlasting life."

God loves you so much that he sacrificed his only son to that we would have the opportunity to see his face. God knows we are sinners, but he gave us a way out when he sent his son to redeem us from our sins. God wants us to live an abundant life not a life that keeps us paralyzed by fear. That is true love.

Athena Jackson

Self-Assessment

Write down a few ways that the wound of rejection has affected your belief system. Examples:

- I am not worthy.
- I am not enough.
- My feelings are not valid.
- I am a failure.
- I must settle because no good man will want me.

Understand that these beliefs are formed because of traumatic events, but in no way does it make these beliefs true.

THE WOUND OF REJECTION

Prayer and Scriptures

Father, in the name of Jesus,

I believe that you are the Son of God and the only way to God the Father. You died on the cross for my sins, and you rose again from the dead. I repent of all my sins, and I forgive all those who have rejected me, hurt me, and failed to show me love Lord, and I trust you also to forgive them and me. I believe Lord that you do accept me. Right now, because of what you did for me on the cross, I acknowledge that I am accepted. I am highly favored. I am the object of your care. I accept myself the way you made me. I am your artistry, and I thank you for what you have created. I am the object of your love and care. I believe that you have begun a good work in me and that you will carry it on to completion until my life ends (Phil. 1:6, 1 Thes. 5:24). Lord, so that your forgiveness can be fully effective in me, I release myself from previous feelings of guilt and from continually going back into the past when I have already asked for your forgiveness. I break any bondage condemning myself and judging myself as being unacceptable to you and others. Release me from these self-destructive thoughts and behaviors, in the precious name of Jesus.

Now, father, I proclaim my release from any dark, evil spirits that have taken advantage of the wounds in my life. Lord, I bind the spirits of rejection, self-rejection, perceived rejection, and fear of rejection, in the blessed name of Jesus Christ. I break the power of the adversary over me, and I command him to leave, in Jesus' name. I renounce any territory that previously given to him, and I joyfully give it back to God. I proclaim my release from dark and evil spirits that have taken advantage of the past wounds in my life. I release my soul to rejoice in the Lord. In Jesus' name, I pray. Amen.

Psalm 94:14 For the Lord will not forsake his people; he will not abandon his heritage;

Psalm 118:22 The stone that the builders rejected has become the cornerstone.

Psalm 139:13-14 For you formed my inward parts; you knitted me together in my mother's womb.

I praise you, for I am fearfully and wonderfully made. Wonderful are your works; my soul knows it very well.

Jeremiah 30:17 For I will restore health to you, and your wounds I will heal, declares the Lord because they have called you an outcast: 'It is Zion, for whom no one cares!'

I praise you, for I am fearfully and wonderfully made. Wonderful are your works; my soul knows it very well.

Jeremiah 30:17 For I will restore health to you, and your wounds I will heal, declares the Lord because they have called you an outcast: 'It is Zion, for whom no one cares!'

Chapter 5

THE WOUND OF ABANDONMENT

The wounds of abandonment are not always visible, but it affects how we behave in our relationships and how we feel internally. The wound of abandonment will cause us to accept the unacceptable in our relationships, hide our voice and spend our lives running from a danger that does not exist.

The wound of abandonment usually develops during childhood when the primary caretaker (usually the mother) is not emotionally available. Emotional unavailability can be because the mother herself suffers from abandonment issues. Children need their mothers to tune in to them emotionally for healthy emotional development. The mother may have been preoccupied, cold, or unable to empathize with her child's emotions. When this happens, the child ends up feeling rejected and alone. The pain of abandonment also happens in situations where a parent is physically absent or doesn't share in parenting. Children can have two parents in the home and suffer from the wounds of abandonment.

The wound of abandonment can also happen in teen years when children are overly criticized, controlled, made to feel inferior or unimportant, or were mistreated. When a child is not adequately cared for, loved, mirrored, and attuned to, the child will feel abandoned regardless of whether the parents are there physically or not. Unfortunately, many parents are simply unaware of the effect they have on their child's emotional health.

Once the wounds of abandonment take root in our subconscious minds, we are bound by the fears formed from those wounds. While the past is in the past, if victims don't uncover the dynamics that led to the wounds, they will be stuck in a never-ending cycle of confusion, just trying to get validation from others. We may not realize we are suffering from the wounds of abandonment or that we suffered from it in our childhood, but we know something is wrong.

While the past is in the past, when people don't uncover the dynamics that led to their emotional wound of abandonment, they will be stuck in a never-ending cycle of confusion, seeking validation from others. Unhealed wounds will set you up to trapped in narcissistic, unhealthy toxic

Athena Jackson

relationships that make you feel unloved, unworthy, and unimportant.

People who usually suffer with abandonment issues are:

- Children of parents who were alcoholics or drug users or were ill or too busy working and could not meet the child's needs for attachment and safety can experience these issues.

- Children of selfish parents who were too focused on their own needs may feel a sense of loss. Scapegoat children almost always feel the loss of a parent's love.

- Children who were separated from their parents and left with other caretakers can feel pushed out and rejected even though there were good reasons for the placement.

- Adopted children often feel abandonment.

- People who felt different from their families or had a biological parent that they did not know or were raised by a stepparent and felt different might have identity issues.

- Sensitive and spiritual children from dysfunctional families feel out of place and different from other family members.

- Divorce and a parent's leaving can create confusion, ideas about being rejected and abandoned, feeling different, and not fitting in.

Here are some symptoms of the fear of abandonment:

- Overly sensitive to criticism
- Difficulty trusting in others
- Trouble making friends unless you can be sure they like you
- Taking extreme measures to avoid rejection or separation
- A pattern of unhealthy relationships
- Getting attached to people too quickly, then moving on just as quickly
- Difficulty committing to a relationship

- Working too hard to please the other person
- Blaming yourself when things don't work out
- Staying in a relationship even if it's not healthy for you
- Clinging or separation anxiety
- Worrying or panic
- Fear of being alone
- Getting sick more often due to stress
- Difficulty concentrating

The first step towards overcoming the fear/wounds of abandonment is to take responsibility for the way you feel. Even though other people's actions might trigger your emotions, you realize that the way you respond to them is up to you.

For example, when you feel insulted, and become angry, you must recognize that, even if the insult was degrading or humiliating, you have a choice about how to react. You can get angry, cry, or storm off. Or, you can search inside yourself and remember that your well-being is not dependent on the opinions of others, then smile and walk away.

Figure out why abandoned is so frightening to you. What particular scenario are you afraid of? If someone left you today, what specific emotion would that generate in you? What thoughts would go through your mind? Getting specific about your fear can help you find ways to combat it. For example, you might fear that if your partner left, you would feel unlovable and lonely. Then speak to your fears and feed them the truth. You are not unlovable, and it's ok to be alone.

Someone walking away from you doesn't define you as less of a person. You are loveable and worthy, whether they stay or leave. Your purpose doesn't change because someone else doesn't see your worth. They can't stop you from becoming the person you were designed to be unless you permit them. You are in control of your life, so don't give power away by allowing your fears to rule your mind. When the fear of abandonment arises, speak to your fear and cast it down with the truth that being alone doesn't mean that you are not unlovable, unimportant or unwanted and it's ok to be alone. The sooner you speak to and conquer the fear of abandonment the less it will plague your mind.

Athena Jackson

THE WOUND OF ABANDONMENT

Prayer and Scriptures

Father in the name of Jesus,

    I renounce the lie and fear of abandonment. I decree and declare its grip and power is broken over my life .Father, you said you would never leave or forsake me (Heb. 13:5), your word also states that "You are with me to the end of the age." (Matthew 28:20) and that if you are with me, who can be against me (Romans 8:31). Father, you also said that though my father and mother forsake me, the Lord will receive me. (Psalm 27:10) Your words tell me that "Then you will know the truth, and the truth will set you free. (John 8:32)

I believe and declare that the truth has set me free from all bondage to the spirit of abandonment. I am accepted in the Beloved. With gratitude in my heart to You, Father, to the Son, and the Holy Spirit, I celebrate the joy and inclusion I am experiencing today and will continue to experience throughout my life in ever-growing measure.

Psalm 27:10-14 (ESV) - For my father and my mother have forsaken me, But the LORD will take me up. Teach me Your way, O LORD, and lead me in a level path Because of my foes. Do not deliver me over to the desire of my adversaries, for false witnesses have risen against me, and such as breathe out violence.

I would have despaired unless I had believed that I would see the goodness of the LORD In the land of the living. Wait for the LORD; Be strong and let your heart take courage; Yes, wait for the LORD.

Joshua 1:9 (ESV) - Have I not commanded you? Be strong and courageous. Do not be frightened, and do not be dismayed, for the Lord your God is with you wherever you go.

Athena Jackson

Psalm 23:1-6 (ESV)-- A Psalm of David. The Lord is my shepherd; I shall not want. He makes me lie down in green pastures. He leads me beside still waters. He restores my soul. He leads me in paths of righteousness for his name's sake. Even though I walk through the valley of the shadow of death, I will fear no evil, for you are with me; your rod and your staff, they comfort me. You prepare a table before me in the presence of my enemies; you anoint my head with oil; my cup overflows.

1 Peter 5:7 (ESV) - Casting all your anxieties on him, because he cares for you.

Romans 8:38-39 (ESV) - For I am sure that neither death nor life, nor angels nor rulers, nor things present nor things to come, nor powers, nor height nor depth, nor anything else in all creation, will be able to separate us from the love of God in Christ Jesus our Lord.

Chapter 6

THE WOUND OF HUMILIATION

The wound of humiliation often appears in people who've experienced a lot of criticism and lack of approval. The humiliation wound generally forms in children whose parents were stringent. These children were often accused of being clumsy, bad, immature, and annoying. Constant criticism can destroy a child's self-esteem. As a result, children develop personality co-dependency. They also create a protective shield to protect themselves from threats that haven't appeared yet. (The mask)

People who suffer from this wound develops the need to please so they wouldn't be criticized or humiliated. The fear of failure is born out of our soul wounds of humiliation. People who wear the mask of shame tend to be kind, pleasant, pleasing, servile, initially self-sacrificing, and charming. People who suffer with this wound make great volunteers because they are always willing to help.

These individuals rarely assert their desires directly, have a tough time saying no, and usually end up doing thankless tasks or things they don't want to do. The wounds humiliation causes individuals to become double-minded; they have a tough time making choices. One moment they are heading left, and when you speak to them again, they are going right. These individuals have little confidence in their ability to make decisions, so they rely on other people to do it for them.

The wound of humiliation breeds feelings of shame and unworthiness. Therefore, the people who suffer from this wound live in a self-defeating cycle. Their lack of self-esteem and self-worth causes them to sabotage and abandon their dreams. They don't believe they are worth it and eventually create situations to stay stuck. They usually won't take the lead but are a great support person and are comfortable being second.

Worry and fear rule the mind of individuals who suffer from the wounds of humiliation. Because of the stress that plagues their minds before taking on a new task, they usually avoid it. They are fear-driven. The fear of being humiliated and shamed is overwhelming to them.

Some of the symptoms of the mask of humiliation are:

- Submissive behavior, and lack of self-assertion (inability to say, "No")

- Intense feelings of shame and disgrace

- Feeling trapped

- Self-destructive behavior patterns (sabotaging success in jobs and relationships, accidents, sexual acting out.)

- Obsessive/compulsive problems, particularly around sex, cleanliness, and orderliness

- Preoccupations with sex, masturbation, pornography and, excretory functions, accompanied by intense guilt, shame, and self-punishment

- An inability to let go of or change repetitive patterns in abusive or ungratifying relationships.

- Inability to tolerate pleasure or success without guilt or anxiety.

The core beliefs of individuals who suffer from the wounds of humiliation

- "I will be loved as long as I submit to the will of others."
- "If I assert my independence, I will be crushed."
- "To get love, I must please others."
- "I can never say no." -
- "I must never express my negativity."
- "I will hurt myself to prevent others from hurting me." -
- "If I feel too much, I will explode." -
- "I am inferior and disgusting because of my negative feelings." -
- "Life is hard and suffering unavoidable."

People who wear the mask of humiliation have some great assets.

- High capacities for pleasure, humor, optimism, playfulness, and joy.

- Genuine supportiveness, strength, and desire to be of service to others.
- An expansive, open heart with deep compassion, genuine kindness, and understanding.
- When released by a strong enough stimulus, there is positive assertiveness and healthy aggression with substantial amounts of energy, the ability to be spontaneously creative in the moment, surrender ego control, and trust the natural order in all things.

Dysfunctional families are shame-based. Parents exhibit the same behaviors towards their children that they experience as children. That is what they know. Parents use shaming tactics when they feel overwhelmed, irritated, or frustrated.

Without educating themselves on how to do constructive parenting and restraining from impulsive angry reactions, they pass the energetic pattern of shame down through the generations. Shaming and blaming may work to stop the misbehavior temporarily, but unfortunately, the costs to the child's self-esteem are tremendous.

Shame is a state of being humiliated by people or circumstances. Disgrace is public humiliation by people or situations. It is not God's will for you to suffer from embarrassment and shame. Every shameful moment that you have experienced as a believer, my God shall give you double restoration in Jesus' name. Shame and disgrace are an affliction of the devil. Therefore, we must tackle it spiritually. Shameful feelings are a threat to our self-integrity, and the fear of shame plagues our minds about being found out by others. This thought is so humiliating that the person goes to all lengths to hide the flawed self. And it gets stuck and put away somewhere deep within. Shame does not have a release valve like tears for sadness or an explosion for anger that helps let it go.

One must identify the root of their humiliation wound and detach from the harsh criticism that it inflicts.

Athena Jackson

One needs to understand that the person or people who were overly critical of them had issues that they passed along to them. They are not under condemnation; God is not punishing them and that he bore all their sins on the cross. I don't know what situations are bringing shame and disgrace in your life; is it barrenness, poverty, sicknesses, a broken relationship, or a broken marriage, but I encourage you to draw closer to your creator so he can reveal his plan and purpose for your life. Understand that he boar every one of your mistakes on the cross, and you have the power to live in freedom from humiliation and shame.

THE WOUND OF HUMILIATION

Prayer and Scriptures

Father, in the name of Jesus, I decree and declare that as of today I am lifted above shame and every inherited curse in my life is now null and void, and every evil door opened in my life, is sealed by the blood of Jesus.

Holy Ghost, I permit you to arrest the spirit of shame and disgrace in every department of my life, in the name of Jesus. Father, I am asking you to baptize me with the spirit of faith that moves mountains in every part of my life, in the name of Jesus. Allow your wisdom to rain in every department of my life. Father grace me as I put on the garment of spiritual boldness and teach me to operate in the spirit of love and forgiveness.

Father give me grace with your favor in every area of my life, in the name of Jesus.

Father, I decree and declare that I am free from the demonic spiritual cage of the enemy, in the name of Jesus. From this day on, I will walk in the freedom awarded to me when Jesus shed his blood for me on Calvary.

Athena Jackson

Father, I come against the spirit of poverty and disconnect myself from financial traps, in the name of Jesus. I uproot every seed of failure in my life and nullify every spirit that causes lack. I cancel and destroy every activity of success polluter, in the name of Jesus. I release financial shame and embarrassment and all evil patterns of failure from my spirit, in the name of Jesus. I come against every poverty activator in every department of my life, in the name of Jesus.

I shall not work for others to eat in the name of Jesus. My blessings, you will not slip off my hands in the name of Jesus. O Lord releases my angels to scatter every evil agent assigned against my family and me in Jesus name.

I command the enemy to lose your grip over my life. Your powers of darkness lose your hold over my life, my marriage, my finances, my health, and my children, right now!!!, in the name of Jesus. Lord, enlarge my territory and silence my enemies in Jesus name.

O Lord, put to shame and disgrace every evil activator pursuing my progress, in the name of Jesus. I decree and declare that every arrow of vagabond spirit fired at me by household wickedness comes out to be sent to dry places, in the name of Jesus.

Every spirit of double-mindedness, you have no place here. Father cast down the spirit of inferiority, backwardness, sickness and disease, obesity, in my life. Father break the generational chain of shame and disgrace over my family and my life in Jesus name.

I come against the spirit of early death and attacks of my organs, skeletal system, and neurological system Jesus name. I lose myself from the bondage of profitless hard work, in the name of Jesus.

Let all evil inquiries about my life be rendered null and void, in the name of Jesus.

Father, I give the dunamis power of the blood of Jesus permission to flow through me and eradicate every spirit that is not of you. Thank you, father, for second chances. In Jesus name, Amen.

Isaiah 43:4 (ESV) - Because you are precious in my eyes and honored, and I love you, I give men in return for you, peoples in exchange for your life.

You are strong.
Habakkuk 3:19 (ESV) - God, the Lord, is my

Athena Jackson

strength; he makes my feet like the deer's; he makes me tread on my high places.

You are chosen.

Isaiah 43:10 (ESV) - You are my witnesses," declares the Lord, "and my servant whom I have chosen,

that you may know and believe me and understand that I am he. Before me no god was formed, nor shall there be any after me.

You are victorious.
Deuteronomy 20:4 (ESV) -The Lord your God is going with you, and he will give you victory.

You are beautiful.
Genesis 1:31(ESV) - God looked at everything he had made, and he was very pleased. The evening passed and morning came—that was the sixth day.

Chapter 7

THE WOUND OF INJUSTICE

According to Lise Bourbeau, The Injustice wound usually forms between the ages of 3 to 5, because nobody helped him to integrate his individuality. This child was most likely raised by cold-hearted unaffectionate, and demanding parents. He didn't learn how to feel with his parents; the performance was more important than feeling good. Thus, it was pretty much impossible for the child to be himself. A person who suffers from the injustice wound is often very demanding, doesn't respect other people's boundaries, and is always stressed out. He is often overly critical of himself and doesn't allow himself to have much fun. He has difficulty seeing what he has done well. A person suffering from the wound of injustice acts with coldness cut off from his senses and thrives by trying to be perfect.

Symptoms of people who suffer from injustice wounds

- Usually Does not realize that he is perceived as cold. The rigid wound ensures that what they are right, while the controlling wants to have the last word on the situation

- Is envious, judging that everyone must have the same to make it fair
- Has difficulty receiving praise, gifts, and rewards (especially receiving more than others because it is not fair)
- Doubt of his choices wants to be sure of the right choice
- Loves order
- Loves to look sexy
- Doesn't admit that he is living problems Has a dry, stiff voice
- Is abrupt in his words and angry
- Finds it difficult to accept his injustice
- Dances very well, he is careful not to make a mistake, takes dance classes easily
- Sits straight, can stiff his legs the one against the other
- Likes the salty stuff over the sweet ones
- Likes to say that he is right, that his life is without problems
- Wants to believe that he has many friends that like him for who he is
  - Fears coldness

Athena Jackson

A person who suffers from wounds of injustice can heal by allowing themselves to make mistakes. They must understand they are perfectly flawed, and that is perfectly ok to be imperfect. God made us all with flaws.

God goes to great lengths to expose the imperfection of the Bible's faith heroes. Abraham was the great model of faith, yet he has his Hagar episode. Moses, was the great Christ-like prophet, has his disqualifying rock incident. David was the king, and he had his affair with Bathsheba. Peter denied Christ three times. God wasn't surprised by any of these men who loved him; he knew they would fail him because they were imperfect. God knows you are imperfect, and he also knows you will make mistakes; this is why he sent his son so that we can be redeemed. God's grace is fresh for us each new morning, so there is no reason to wallow in your imperfection.

When you fail, get up, dust yourself off, and continue to walk in excellence, not perfection.

God desires for us to be free from pride and fear. He wants us to live in the freedom of knowing that he has our past, present, and future perfection issues wholly covered. Through the blood of Jesus, you are free! You are free to follow Jesus imperfectly.

Here are a few strategies for dealing with the wound of injustice (perfectionism):

1. Jot down things that are important to you and why: The things you list are essential but examining *why* it is even more revealing.

2. Avoid competitive environments: Do you have to be the best at your church group or fitness club? When you go to a place, do you feel peace, or do you find yourself criticizing others? Do you only want to win and bend others to your will?

3. Don't be afraid to admit – and *show* – your weakness: This is very hard for perfectionists. Pray for this grace. Remember that failure allows you to learn and grow.

Athena Jackson

THE WOUND OF INJUSTICE

Prayer and Scriptures

Father, in the name of Jesus,

I relinquish my need to be perfect along with my fear of failure to you. I ask you to unravel the cords of perfectionism over my mind and heart and soul.

Today I surrender to you my life entirely and renounce every spirit and wound that does not align with your word. I relinquish all religion, tradition, all perfectionism, all pride and discontentment, all ego and vanity, all frustration, intolerance, impatience, and condemnation with others and myself, and I thank you that you are removing them from my life; that you will give me abundant grace to overcome all the works of the enemy that have hindered me.

Uproot and heal all the negative experiences in my life and help me to forgive those that treated me with perfectionism. Help me, father, to worship and praise you in all things.

Give me a grateful heart, a heart of thanksgiving before you.

Father, continue to pour LOVE in me and set me free from all my fears. I ask you for more wisdom, knowledge, and understanding as I start on this new journey to trust you. From this day forward, I will lean not to my understanding but in all my ways acknowledge you so that you may direct my past. Father, as I shed off my old perfectionist belief system, I ask you to grace me as I adopt a new healthy belief system that is grounded in your word.   Thank you for your grace and mercy. Thank you for being patient with me and offering me a new opportunity to begin again in Jesus Mighty Name, Amen.

Athena Jackson

Hebrews 11:6 (ESV)

And without faith, it is impossible to please him, for whoever would draw near to God must believe that he exists and that he rewards those who seek him.

Galatians 1:10 (ESV) - For am I now seeking the approval of man or God? Or am I trying to please man? If I were still trying to please man, I would not be a servant[a] of Christ.

1 John 4:18-19 (ESV)- There is no fear in love, but perfect love casts out fear. For fear has to do with punishment, and whoever fears has not been perfected in love. We love because he first loved us.

Chapter 8

THE WOUND OF BETRAYAL

Individuals who suffer from the wound of betrayal are usually very controlling and often suffer from the wound of abandonment because their greatest fear is separation.

Lise Bourbeau states that the wound of betrayal is usually formed in childhood when a parent (generally of the opposite sex) doesn't follow through with commitments. For example, take a mother who ponds her son off on a grandparent so she can be with her financially well-off man. This child grows up, and he now attracts women with money. He may fall for them for a while; however, at some point when he is ready to leave the relationship, he creates problems for his partner so she will want to walk away. He may repeat this cycle repetitively. This child's fear of separation and lack of attention causes him to put on the mask of the controller.

Controllers often use words like I am capable, I can do it by myself, or Do you understand? They have high expectations and are very moody. They are master manipulators and act fast. Controllers love being in love, and once this feeling subsides, they will make you want to leave them. They do this, so they don't feel like they have betrayed anyone.   Controllers are charming, not just in intimate relationships but in every area of their lives. They make the best sons, sons-in-law, friends, and co-workers.

Controllers do not like to be wrong or questioned as this a major strike to their ego, and according to them, their way is right. They will lie and will make excuses to accommodate their lies.

This wound, like the other ones, is rooted in fear. People try to control outcomes in fear of what will happen if they don't have control. Relinquishing the need to be in control will result in enjoying more joy, freedom, peace, connection, and support. God does not require you to be in control. He wants to be in control. For a controlling person to let go of their controlling nature, they have to heal and forgive the painful experience that formed the fear of abandonment. Let's use the above example of the mother who dumped her son on his grandmother so that she can be with her well off boyfriend. The son needs to forgive the mother as well as the boyfriend so he can heal the fears that plague his mind.

Let God be God. Learning to let go and trust God may be challenging at first, but the more it's practiced, the better at it you will become. You will come to learn that God will never fail you or forsake you. Understand that God knows

Athena Jackson

THE WOUND OF BETRAYAL

Prayer and Scriptures

Father, In the name of Jesus,

I ask you to heal my wounds of betrayal. Calm my fears of separation and my fears of the unknown. I confess that I often allow myself to be controlled by my desires and impulses rather than by Your Spirit. Father, I repent for myself and my generational line. I repent for all manipulation that resulted in the spirit of Jezebel, the spirit of control, envy, and jealousy of others. I ask for forgiveness for injuring others with my words and actions and for using others for selfish gain.

Father, I decree and declare that all curses and assignments of the spirit of control over myself and my generational line are broken. Remove all ungodly spiritual beings and evil networks connected to me and empowered by the sins of my ancestors. Restore to me and my family line all that the enemy has stolen. Restore health, finances, and godly authority. I ask that you heal and restore broken relationships.

Father, I surrender my need to be in control and choose to walk in the protective armor of you. Bless me as I learn to walk in grace, humbleness, and mercy. As I adopt the heart of forgiveness, I will bless those who persecute me. Father teach me to become patient, loving, and kind as I learn to be humble. Father grace me as I learn to lift, honor, and edify others. It's not my will, but thy will be done in my life. I welcome the opportunity for you to make me over again as I set out to heal the wounds of my soul. Thank you for being a forgiving and loving God. I appreciate the opportunity to start over, knowing that you are in control. In Jesus name, amen.

Romans 8:28 (ESV)- And we know that for those who love God, all things work together for good, for those who are called according to his purpose.

Jeremiah 29:11 (ESV) - For I know the plans I have for you, declares the Lord, plans for welfare and not for evil, to give you a future and a hope

Matthew 6:34 (ESV)- Therefore do not be anxious about tomorrow, for tomorrow will be anxious for itself. Sufficient for the day is its trouble.

Athena Jackson

Isaiah 41:10 (ESV)- Fear not, for I am with you; be not dismayed, for I am your God; I will strengthen you, I will help you, I will uphold you with my righteous right hand.

Soul Cleanse Day *1*

Detoxing Negative Thought Patterns

    Your most dominant thoughts shape your world, these thoughts are stored in your subconscious (the part of the mind of which one is not fully aware, but which influences one's actions and feelings) mind. People act and react in response to how they think. Therefore, most emotionally damaged individuals operate out of a limiting belief system. Their traumatic experiences left a major imprint in their consciousness, and this imprint influences their negative thought patterns and therefore compromises their belief system.

    Proverbs 23:7 lets us know that " as someone thinks within himself so is he," so what you continuously think about and how you think, shows up in who you are and what you become. If you consistently think you can't achieve something, then you won't achieve it.

    Your subconscious mind is like a storage bank, think of it as an I Cloud.

Athena Jackson

Your subconscious mind is the master program of your conscious mind, and it ensures you are operating according to the way it is programmed. Your reasoning, emotions, and thoughts from your childhood experiences all contribute to programming the subconscious mind. The way you think act and respond is all being nourished from the master program of your subconscious mind. Your subconscious mind will communicate to your conscious mind," you are not wired for this." Right here is where most people choose to retract back to their comfort zones and fall back into their familiar patterns. When fear arises, it a sign that your subconscious mind is activated. If your damaged emotions are the master program of your subconscious mind, it will continue to feed your negative thought patterns and keep you in a cycle of defeat. Below are some examples of damaged emotions

- **Anger** - intense feelings of hostility, wrath, powerless.

- **Abandonment** - feelings of being forsaken, left behind, cast off & stranded.

- **Betrayal** - Feelings of Disloyalty & broken trust.

- **Bitterness** - Feelings of Anger & resentment.

- **Defensiveness** - Feelings of being guarded, preconceived attracts.

- **Fear** - Feelings of Anxiety, terror, panic.

- **Failure** - Feeling of being unsuccessful, defeated, stuck, blocked.

- **Criticism** - Feelings of disapproval, condemnation, attack.

- **Resentfulness** - feelings of bitterness, anger, and unforgiveness.

- **Hopelessness** - feeling of being stuck, defeated, now way out

- **Regret** - the feeling of remorse or guilt.

Athena Jackson

- **Pride** - feelings of being better than, selfish, and arrogant.

- **Shame** - feelings of humiliation and embarrassment.

- **Guilt** - the feeling of remorse & regret

- **Stubbornness** - refusal to corporate, headstrong.

- **Rejection** - feelings of being unwanted, discarded, forsaken.

- **Regret** - feelings of disappointment, sadness, guilt.

- **Loneliness** - the feeling of being alone, unloved, unwanted.

- **Unworthy** - feelings of being invaluable, worthless.

- **Insecure** -feelings of "not enough, low self-confidence

- **Inferior** - Feelings of unworthiness & less than.

Which of these damaged emotions could you identify with?

_____
_____
_____
_____

Now let's look at some of the negative thought patterns that accompany these emotions.

- People always leave me
- Why do people judge me all the time?
- People never say nice things about me.
- I'm not good enough /smart enough/ I'm not enough.
- Things never work out in my favor.
- I always fail at everything
- There is no need to get my hopes up.

Athena Jackson

- Why am I here?
- No one wants me.
- Everyone only looks out for themselves.
- They don't care about me
- I can't.
- I give up.
- I hate them/him/her.
- God hates me.
- No one has ever had my back.
- I will never amount to anything.
- That is what they get.
- I will never measure up.
- I'm not pretty/ handsome enough.
- If I only had…. I would be better off.
- I don't deserve it.
- I can't forgive.

Each one of these thought patterns was shaped from a deeper source. These thoughts are just the fruit from experiences that produced these feelings. For instance, take a child who was physically abused; this child would have a few of these thought patterns operating at the same time. Anger, fear, anxiety, resentment, bitterness, defensive, and unworthy would probably among those thought patterns. This child subconscious mind is being programmed, and by the time he/she becomes an adult, his/her mind is already fully programmed.

By the time I was an adult, I was wired to believe I wasn't worthy. The wound of rejection, humiliation, and abandonment controlled my life. I was a master procrastinator, easily overwhelmed, and felt inferior to other people. My decisions were slaves to the fears of my soul wounds. I was always waiting for some trauma to occur. I lived my life in complete terror of being rejected. I was plagued with the fear of people walking out of my life. My damaged emotions of "not being good enough" fed this fear. Although I longed and dreamed of becoming who I am today, I couldn't see it back then, and when I would try and step out of my comfort zone, fear and shame paralyzed me and snatched me back. All this was a result of my unaddressed traumatic experiences. My thoughts and emotions formed from these experiences were programming my subconscious mind, and eventually, I became enslaved to my negative thought patterns.

Athena Jackson

When I decided to heal from my damaged emotions, I knew it was vital that I re-train my subconscious mind by consistently feeding it the truth.

After years of doing good deeds in the church and my community, I realized that I didn't truly know God, I only knew of him. My negative thought patterns caused me to become separated from him and my purpose. My first task was to learn more about my creator. I knew the secret to my healing was to understand who my creator was. I needed to develop a closer relationship with him. I wanted to know who he was? What he likes and dislikes, what his purpose was for my life.

I found all these answers in the word of God. Once I began to know him, I discovered that he has never created anything that wasn't valuable. Everything he touched had a meaning and purpose. Therefore, I was precious, and I was worthy of being loved. I came to know that God had not rejected me, or was he ashamed of me for my mistakes. As a matter of fact, he had plans for my pain, he began to heal my broken pieces, and I finally began to see myself differently. Today he is using my testimony to heal other women.

God wants to give you the same experience through the renewing of your mind. (Romans 12:2) God wants to change your mind about who you are, and the only way to do that is by getting to know him. God wants us to be still and know that he is God. Being still and getting into his presence through prayer, meditation, and the reading of his word. The bible commands us in 2 Corinthians 10:5 to *bring every thought into captivity and cast down wicked imaginations*. He also tells us in Philippians 4:8 "Whatever is noble, whatever is right, whatever is pure, whatever is lovely, whatever is admirable—if anything is excellent or praiseworthy—think about such things.

When fear and anxiety begin to sing in your mind, read scriptures on fear and anxiety. When people hurt you, read scriptures on forgiveness, combat your negative patterns with the word of God, and watch how you began to view yourself differently. You will start to embrace God's plan for your life.

Athena Jackson

DETOXING NEGATIVE THOUGHT PATTERNS

Prayer and Scriptures

Father, in the name of Jesus, I come before you asking you to forgive my unbelief. Forgive me for allowing my past painful experiences to control my belief system. Grace me, father, as I learn the thoughts you have for me. Father, I decree and declare I will no longer speak 'death' over myself with my negative self-talk. I cast down the spirit of fear and the wounds that accompany them. No longer will gossip and criticism be my language. Today Lord, we ask you to turn my negative thoughts and words into dust and let them fall to the ground as I learn to hide your word in my heart. I cast down negative word curses I've spoken over my life and the word curses of others. Father today is a new day, and I will begin today – now – to SPEAK LIFE over myself and others in Jesus Name.

1st Peter 2:9 (ESV) - But ye are a chosen race, a royal priesthood, a holy nation, a people for his own possession, that you may proclaim the excellencies of him who called you out of darkness into his marvelous light.

Romans 8:35-39 (ESV) - Who shall separate us from the love of Christ? Shall tribulation, or distress, or persecution, or famine, or nakedness, or danger, or sword?

1 Corinthians 3:16(ESV) - Do you not know that you are God's temple and that God's Spirit dwells in you?

Ephesians 3:6 (ESV) - This mystery is that the Gentiles are fellow heirs, members of the same body, and partakers of the promise in Christ Jesus through the gospel.

Ephesians 3:20(ESV)-Now to him who is able to do far more abundantly than all that we ask or think, according to the power at work within us.

Athena Jackson

Soul Cleanse Day *2*

DESTROYING LIMITING BELIEFS

Belief according to Merriam-Webster

1: a state or habit of mind in which trust or confidence is placed in some person or thing.

2: something that is accepted, considered to be true, or help as an opinion: something believed.

Limiting Belief

Something you believe becomes your truth, and that belief limits you from making progress. These beliefs could be about you, the world, or other people. Limiting beliefs hinder your growth and stop you from reaching your full potential. They hide your gifts from you and hinder you from receiving them from other people. A few examples of limiting beliefs are:

- I am imperfect
- I am worthless
- I can't …
- I am nonexistent

- I am inadequate

Look at how limiting beliefs shape your world.

Limiting belief: I am Imperfect

Negative Core Belief: "There is something wrong with me."

Compensating Personality: "I must be perfect. I have to prove to everyone that there is nothing wrong with me. *"If I do it perfectly enough, I will be healed."*

Limiting belief: I am Worthless

Negative Core Belief: "I have no value."

Compensating Personality: "I must prove I am not worthless. I must prove that I have worth and value." This personality overcompensates to be accepted. And constantly seek validation. Flattery and is co-dependent. *"If I give to others, I will be healed."*

Limiting Belief: I Cannot Do Enough

Negative Core Belief: "I cannot do, decide, or act. This person suffers from "I am not enough syndrome and continuously seeks approval.

Compensating Personality: "I must prove that I can do, decide, and act by becoming an overachiever." This person becomes grandiose - about what it can do and often is arrogant and cocky. *"If I accomplish enough, I will be healed."*

Athena Jackson

Limiting Belief: I am Inadequate

Negative Core Belief: "I am inadequate. I am stupid. I do not know enough."

Compensating Personality: "I must prove that I am not inadequate. I must prove that I am adequate and smart." This personality struggles between feeling stupid and tries to be overly adequate by being over-analytic and over-reasonable. *"If I am smart enough, I will be healed."*

Limiting Belief: I am Non-Existent

Negative Core Belief: "I don't exist. I am nothing. I have nothing." This false core develops earlier than others - often in utero - and is more deeply embedded in the body than any of the other False Core Selves.

This False Core believes, "I am nothing. I am empty. I don't know." This type of person is unsuitable for Buddhist (no-self) and non-dual spiritual practices because they reinforce the False Core assumptions.

Compensating Personality: "I must prove that I am something, have something, and that I exist." This personality "thinks" feelings and does not feel them. This could be because of rejection from the mother in utero. This personality dissociates from feelings early and becomes an over-observer as a defense. *"If I disappear enough, I will be healed."*

Your emotions play a significant role in how we react and respond to situations. Your emotions also play a role in how you feel. So, it is safe to say when you think different or better, you feel different/ better.

Your belief system shows up in how you are living your life; it also shows up in your words. There is a saying that if you change your mind, you change your destiny. I found this to be very real in my own life. When my mind changed, so did my life.

Take a few minutes to jot down a few of your limiting beliefs

1._____
_____

2._____
_____

3._____
_____

Write down your Compensating Personality attached to that belief. (Use the examples above)

1._____
_____

2._____
_____

3._____
_____

Athena Jackson

Limiting beliefs are not facts. I used to believe that people would label me if I showed my true colors and that I had to earn happiness. I didn't realize that I could just choose happiness. So, I was hard on myself and wore a mask around certain people. Once I decided to change my thinking patterns, yes, I had to make a conscious choice to change my mind, I re-wrote my limiting beliefs. The most powerful tool you have in your mind, and it is the enemy's job to fight you in your mind. As long as he has a foothold over your mind, you will continue to be defeated. He wants to keep you in bondage to your limiting beliefs so that you stay stressed, frustrated, and angry, and sick.

You can't take your old mindset into a new lifestyle. Make up in your mind that you will not waste another day on an unproductive mindset. You have the power to change your mind. When you decide to change your mind, you are electing to change your destiny. The only person who can initiate the change in your mind is YOU!

DESTROYING LIMITING BELIEFS

Prayer and Scriptures

Psalms 91 Inspired Prayer

Father, in the name of Jesus,

Today, I choose to dwell in the secret place of the most high, And so I abide in the shadow of the almighty. Today I say of the *lord* **YOU ARE MY REFUGE AND MY FORTRESS MY GOD; IN YOU I PUT MY TRUST**. Surely you will deliver me from the snare of the fowler and the noisome pestilence. You cover me with your feathers, and under your wings, I trust. Father, your truth is my shield and buckler; therefore, I am not afraid of the terror by night nor for that flies by day. I am not afraid of the pestilence that walks in darkness; nor for the destruction that wastes at noonday.

      Father, you said that a thousand should fall at my side and ten thousand at my right hand, but it NOT come by me. Only with my eyes do I look and see the reward of the wicked. Because I have made you my refuge and my fortress, even the highest, my habitation; No evil befalls me, nor does any plague come nigh my dwelling. Father, I am

Athena Jackson

protected because you have given your angels charge over me to keep me in all my ways. They bear me up in their hands, I tread upon the lion and the cobra, and the serpent I trample on. Father, I have set my love upon you, and you delivered me. You set me in high places because I know your name. Father, I call upon you, and you answer me. You are with me in times of trouble, and you deliver and honor me. With long life, you satisfy me and show me your salvation.

Father today, I renounce the spirit of fear and the limiting beliefs that accommodate them. From his day forward, I will rest in your word. Thank you for your grace and mercy and the opportunity to operate in the belief system that I am who You say I am. Father, you created me in your image, and I accept the fact that I am limitless, and I can walk in the greatness you set before me.

In Jesus name. Amen

Philippians 4:13 (ESV)- I can do all this through him who gives me strength.

2 Timothy 1:7(ESV) - **For** the Spirit God gave us does not make us timid but gives us power, love, and **self**-discipline.

Hebrews 4:16 (ESV) - Let us then approach God's throne of grace with **confidence**, so that we may receive mercy and find grace to help us in our time of need.

Hebrews 12:11(ESV) - For the moment all discipline seems painful rather than pleasant, but later it yields the peaceful fruit of righteousness to those who have been trained by it.

Athena Jackson

Soul Cleanse Day 3
THE ROOT OF BITTERNESS

The root of bitterness starts with anger, then turns into grudges. When you are offended or disappointed by others and allow the hurt to germinate in your heart, bitterness and resentment will take root. An unforgiving spirit and generally negative, critical attitudes, and jealousy are sinful and self-defeating. You are essentially robbing yourself from peace, joy, and happiness. (**Ephesians 4:31-32**) Says, "*Let all bitterness and wrath and anger and clamor and slander be put away from you, along with all malice. Be kind to one another, tenderhearted, forgiving one another, as God in Christ forgave you.*"

Dr. Carsten Worsch, of Concordia University in Montreal, explains that resentment and bitterness interfere with our body's hormonal systems. This interference causes a majorly damaging effect through our entire body, much like extreme stress. Dr. Worsch also has noted that these negative emotions interfere with our immune system as well, causing us to be susceptible to illness and disease. The negativity can even cause heart problems, according to Dr. Charles Raison of the University of Arizona Health Sciences.

Here Are a few signs you may be bitter:

You rehearse conversations or experiences in your mind over and over.

Whether it's past a conversation or experience, you bring the past into the present every time you replay it in your mind. You continue to give life to negative thoughts and emotions that are attached to your experience. Jesus came to redeem our pasts, even the parts that are not a result of our sin. However, when you rehearse our history, you are not allowing him to do that.

Athena Jackson

Philippians 3:13 encourages us to "Forget *what is behind and straining toward what is ahead. Let it go and move on.*"

You find joy in people's failures

You get happy when someone you are bitter towards faces some hardship. Celebrating other people's misfortune is malice, and it is sinful. Malice shows that we are harboring bitterness in our hearts. How do you feel when other people jump up and down and have a celebration because you are going through rough times? I found that when I pray for people who hurt me, especially when they are down, it helps me to release those toxic emotions I have toward them.

You feel the need to belittle other people.

When someone hurts us, we tend to find validation in slandering that person's name. While it is ok to become angry, the bible says, "Be angry, and sin not, down let the sun go down on your anger." (Ephesians 4:26) It's not ok to spread discord about this person. A person may not realize they offended or hurt you. The best solution is to go to that person and let them know how the incident made you feel. Don't attack them, take responsibility for your feelings, and move forward. If confronting them is not an option, express your emotions in a journal, or to someone who can offer direction and positive feedback.

You are unhappy and get jealous of others.

When people are unhappy and insecure, they cringe when they see other people winning. They find it challenging to celebrate other people. Unhappiness comes from unforgiveness and bitterness.

When you catch yourself despising someone else's accomplishments, stop and intentionally celebrate them. Also, take note of the negative thoughts that came to the surface, then figure out why their achievement caused those thoughts. For instance, someone gets a promotion; it strikes a chord in you. Is it because their development makes you feel less accomplished? Are there areas in your life you know you can be doing better but refuse or too scared to step up and do the work. Have you been working hard in some areas and not getting the results you desire? Answer those questions, own your issues.

This list goes on, but you can defeat bitterness with forgiveness. The sooner to choose to let go of these non-productive negative thoughts of your past painful experiences, the sooner you will find the joy and happiness you deserve. You have the power to control your thoughts, when unhealthy thoughts arise, deal with it, and let it go.

You can be affected physically, mentally, spiritually, and emotionally as a result of bitterness and resentment. Your relationships will always suffer.

Get a gratitude journal; daily write down three things to which you are thankful. You can be grateful for waking up, being in your right mind, and the mobility of your limbs. Jot down your painful experiences as you navigate through, note your thoughts and feelings don't hold them in. Bitterness grows when we allow our negative emotions fester.

Focus on making your life better. You can't change the past and the hurt and offenses caused by your offenders, so don't spend the rest of your life pondering on them and praying for their downfalls. What you wish on others has a way of coming back to you. Let it go.

Soul Cleanse Day 4

THE HEART OF GRATITUDE

The Hear of gratitude helps to detox negative thought patterns and emotions. Robert A. Emmons, Ph. D., who researched gratitude and well-being, confirms that gratitude increases happiness and reduces depression. Instead of focusing on what you don't have, being grateful for where you are now, and the resources you have available to you will keep you from comparing yourself to other people. Many people fall into the rut of focusing and keeping up with the Joneses that they forget to thank god for their own homes and family.

A heart of gratitude will keep you from falling into depression about your past experiences. When you thank God for your lessons and mistakes and leverage them to grow, it's hard to stay depressed and live in mental anguish about the past. A heart of gratitude enables you to make lemonade from the lemons thrown at you. You will be able to bounce back much quicker when life hasn't been so kind. Thank God for your hard times because the storms build and shape your character, revealing your inner strength along with other hidden attributes you never knew you had.

It is easy to be grateful when you land your dream job or buy your dream house. The true test of gratitude is proven when you lose everything and still thank God for the breath you have in your body, for the birds in the air, and the fish in the sea. The heart of gratitude requires discipline; it requires you to dig deep when you are overwhelmed with the cares of this world and still be grateful. Practicing gratitude is resting and being assured that God will ultimately redeem every horrible situation in this life or the next

. *"He will wipe every tear from their eyes. There will be no more death' or mourning or crying or pain, for the old order of things has passed away."* (Revelation 21:4).

Gratitude requires humility because it exposes our need for God in our lives. It is a heart condition that acknowledges that without God, we are nothing, and because of him, we have everything we need? Psalms 100:4 commands us, *"Enter His gates with thanksgiving and His courts with praise; give thanks to Him and praise His name."* In gratitude, we give God thanks, not just for material things but for him.

Athena Jackson

THE HEART OF GRATITUDE

Prayer and Scriptures

Father, in the name of Jesus,

Despite my fooling ways, failures, and mistakes, you still call me your child. I praise and thank you for the many and great blessings that you have showered over us all, despite our foolish ways and sinful and prideful nature. You are a gracious and merciful God who is mindful of me even when I couldn't see my worth. Thank you, Father, for your unconditional and everlasting love. May I grow more and more to be like you. I ask that you continue to guide and teach me in all that I say and do and that I may do all according to your will. I ask you to continue to pour out bountiful blessings and mercy on me as I surrender to your will for my life. I love and appreciate you for who you are. For you are my provider, protector, deliverer, way maker, miracle worker, and a promise keeper. You are Abba, my father, and I am forever grateful for your unfailing love for me. In Jesus name, Amen

Ephesians 5:20 (ESV) - "thanks always for all things to God the Father in the name of our Lord Jesus Christ."

I Thessalonians 5:18 (ESV) "in everything give thanks for this is the will of God in Christ Jesus for you."

Colossians 3:17 (ESV), "whatever you do in word or deed, do all in the name of the Lord Jesus, giving thanks to God the Father through Him."

Psalm 107:21-22 (ESV) Oh, that men would give thanks to the LORD for His goodness, and for His wonderful works to the children of men! Let them sacrifice [or offer] the sacrifices of thanksgiving and declare His works with rejoicing.

Athena Jackson

Soul Cleanse Day 5
ACKNOWLEDGE YOUR PAIN

    The coping mechanism I used to manage my emotional wounds was to bury them. They would surface from time to time, and when this happened, I would find a way to suppress them again. The pain of dealing with those emotions was overwhelming, and I didn't want to deal with it. It was much easier to make excuses for the different experiences in my life, then to accept them for what they were. Suppressing my emotions would cause me to become vulnerable to toxic, unhealthy environments. Rather than deal with the discomfort of confrontation, I chose instead to bury my pain and anger and leave it to accumulate. Little did I know I was making things worse.

    The problem with suppressing your pain is that when we don't effectively manage our hurt feelings, over time, we tend to alter our behavior and do whatever it takes to keep from appearing vulnerable and avoid being hurt again. Over time, those emotions you've been suppressing and could erupt when unexpectantly and serves as a tipping point, and you suddenly experience overwhelming feelings of hurt and anger without really understanding why.

The first step in detoxing is acknowledging your pain emotionally, which is also known as confrontation. Here is where you stop running from your pain. Now is the time to bring your pain to the surface, and express your feelings about your experiences, permit yourself to be angry, and release those emotions. Below is an exercise that allows you to have a heart to heart conversation about the event and how it made you feel.

Athena Jackson

There is a beauty in pain because you risked, you loved, and you allowed yourself to feel. Hurt will be the thing that brings you to yourself, before and after the pain—before; there is happiness; after, there is transcendence. Pain is a part of life, not something to run from, to escape. The pain will find you somehow, and to go through its cleansing fire will be one of the most real things that can happen to you in your life if you let it.

In this exercise, you will need a piece of paper for each person involved in your traumatic event, including yourself. On each piece of paper, write the name of the person who hurt you in large letters (feel free to use pictures) and tape their names on the wall in alignment with your eyes. Put the names in chronological order of who hurt you first. When I did this exercise, I started with my father because he abandoned me when I was four years old.

I Healed on Purpose

Next, stand in front of the person's name and recall the event. Tell them how it made you feel and the impact it had on your life. If you were a child, allow your inner child to speak to them. (*When I talked to my father, who is deceased, and expressed how I didn't believe he didn't love me, and I figured it was because I wasn't good enough to be his daughter. I told him that if he were around, my violators wouldn't have been so free to take advantage of his little girl.*) I allowed the little girl to speak to my father). I also talked to each person that sexually violated me, the people who hurt me. Do this for everyone that hurt you. Scream, yell, and cry if you must, but release those emotions. Don't try and contact these people. Remember, this is about freeing your feelings. After you complete this task, leave those names tapped on the wall. You will need them for the next lessons.

Athena Jackson

When you get to your name, take your name and tape to the mirror. Face yourself in the mirror, look yourself in the eye, and express your feelings about the mistakes you made as a result of your past wounds. Afterward, step back and take a few deep breaths then recite these affirmations.

- I release this pain from my life.
- These memories will no longer have control over my life.
- I release all these unrelenting, painful thoughts and emotions that are a result of these events.
- I denounce any self-sabotaging beliefs that I formed, resulting from these events.
- I choose to walk in the freedom that forgiveness offers me.
- I want to forgive everyone, including myself.
- I take full responsibility for the mistakes I made as a result of my past.
- My past does not dictate my future, and my future looks good on me.
- I am victorious, and no, I am longer bound by the painful events of my past.

You have just made a major impact on your healing journey acknowledging these painful events and the people associated with them.

Healing takes time.

Some offenses are unintentional and easily forgiven once they are acknowledged, while more severe, profound wounds take time. The willingness to go through the process of self-discovery, with the understanding that sometimes the only way to heal a deep-seated soul wound, is letting go of a situation or relationship that no longer serves you.

Honoring your pain isn't a sign of weakness; it takes courage and strength to allow yourself to explore your painful emotions. Indeed, the process of acknowledging your feelings and working through them will leave you feeling more confident and freer than ever since you will no longer be lugging around the baggage of those long-buried emotions.

Athena Jackson

ACKNOWLEDGING YOUR PAIN

Prayer and Scriptures

Father, in the name of Jesus, I come to you with a feeling of shame and emotional hurt. I confess my transgressions to you continually unfolding the past until all is told. You are faithful and just to forgive me and to cleanse me of all unrighteousness. You are my hiding place, and you, Lord, preserve me from trouble. You surround me with songs and shouts of deliverance. I have chosen life. According to your word, you saw me while I formed in my mother's womb; and on the authority of your word, I was wonderfully made. Now I am Your handiwork, recreated in Christ Jesus.

Father, you have delivered me from the spirit of fear, and I shall not be ashamed. Neither shall I be confounded and depressed. You gave me beauty for ashes, the oil of joy for mourning, and the garment of praise for the spirit of heaviness that I might be called a tree of righteousness, the planting of the Lord, that you might be glorified. I speak out in psalms, hymns, and spiritual songs, offering praise with my voice and making melody with all my heart to You. Just as David did in 1 Samuel 30:6, I encourage myself in you.

    I believe in you, Lord, who raised Jesus from the dead. He was betrayed and put to death due to my misdeeds and raised to secure my (acquittal), [absolving me from all guilt before You]. Father, you anointed Jesus and sent Him to bind up and heal my broken heart and liberate me from the shame of my youth and the imperfections of my caretakers. In His name, I choose to forgive all those who have wronged me in any way. You will not leave me without support as I complete the forgiveness process. I take comfort and am encouraged and confidently say, "The Lord is my Helper; I will not be seized with alarm…What can man do to me?" (Heb. 13:6).

    Lord search my innermost parts of my being, expose shame and emotional pain. My past can't compare to the glory that is about to be revealed to me and in me and for me. My faith in you will never disappoint, delude, or shame me, for your love has been poured out in my heart through the Holy Spirit.

In Jesus name, I pray, Amen.

-Prayers That Avail Much-

Athena Jackson

Romans 5:3-5(ESV) - More than that, we rejoice in our sufferings, knowing that suffering produces endurance, and endurance produces character, and character produces hope, and hope does not put us to shame because God's love has been poured into our hearts through the Holy Spirit.

Psalms 147:3(ESV) - He healeth the broken in heart, and bindeth up their wounds.

Jeremiah 30:17(ESV) - For I will restore health unto thee, and I will heal thee of thy wounds, saith the LORD; because they called thee an Outcast, [saying], This [is] Zion, whom no man seeketh after.

Psalms 142:7(ESV) - Bring my soul out of prison, that I may praise thy name: the righteous shall compass me about; for thou shalt deal bountifully with me.

Psalms 34:18 (ESV)- The LORD [is] nigh unto them that are of a broken heart; and saveth such as be of a contrite spirit.

Psalms 30:2 (ESV) -O LORD my God, I cried unto thee, and thou hast healed me.

Soul Cleanse Day 6

THE GIFT OF FORGIVENESS

Forgiveness is one of the characteristics of God. The reason we can repent from our sins and he forgives them is because of the love he has for us. God's desire is for us to sit in heaven with him one day, so he sent his son to die on the cross for us so that we would have the opportunity to have a fresh start. He gave us the gift of forgiveness. God wants us to operate under the same love that he has towards us. Think of how many times you disappointed God by making mistakes or even when you've done something you knew he wouldn't be proud of, but you chose to do it regardless. God still forgives you when you ask for it. He is a forgiving God. In Matthew 18:21-22, it says, "Then came Peter to him, and said, Lord, how oft shall my brother sin against me, and I forgive him? Till seven times? **Jesus saith unto him, I say not unto thee, Until seven times: but, Until seventy times seven.**"

Compassion is the key to forgiveness; it is the very reason God sent his Son to die on the cross. To forgive, you have to be compassionate read. Instead, it is abuse, abandonment, or rejection; you have to rise above your offender no matter what the offense. My father passed before I eventually forgave him. His alcoholism and rejection used to cringe my very spirit. One day I realized that he was emotionally damaged; he was worse off than I was, and that hurting people hurt people. He didn't have it within himself to love me the way I needed to be loved; he didn't love himself. Did that mean I deserved abandonment, no, it didn't, because he couldn't give me what he didn't have?

Once I came to this realization, I was able to release my father and forgive him.

There are times when we make mistakes, and we need forgiveness, and just as we need others to find it in their hearts (compassion) to forgive us, we must forgive.

Forgiveness is a conscious, deliberate decision to release feelings of resentment or vengeance toward a person or group who has harmed you; Forgiveness does not mean forgetting, nor does it mean condoning or excusing offenses. Forgiveness is a gift of happiness that you give yourself. Holding on to resentment, anger, revenge, or any other feeling that follows unforgiveness only brings harm to you.

People will move on with their lives, but unless you release the pain from your hurtful event, you set yourself up to suffer emotionally, physically, mentally, and spiritually. Unforgiveness is a part of the devil's character, and if he can cause you to keep recalling a painful event and harbor toxic emotions, he eventually takes ownership of your heart.

Matthew 6:15 tells us that "But if you do not forgive others their sins, your Father will not forgive your sins." The bible also says, "Blessed are the merciful, for they will be shown mercy." (Matthew 5:7)

    Until I chose to forgive the people that hurt me, I suffered. Those toxic emotions ran deep, and I was under loads of stress. Unforgiveness caused the unnecessary burden of trying to be accepted, and please everyone. My blood pressure skyrocketed; arthritis kept me in pain. I endured heart failure and overactive thyroid.

Athena Jackson

I realized that once I started my healing journey and began to make peace with my past, most of those issues begin to disappear. The secret to my healing process was adopting the spirit of forgiveness.

Luke 6:27-28 Jesus tells us to love our enemies and do good to them who hate us. He also says to bless them that curse you and pray for them that which despitefully use you. In verse 35, he tells us that if we do this that our reward will be great, and we shall be the children of the highest. Your blessing and breakthrough are contingent on your willingness to forgive. The heart that forgives is a rewarding lifestyle. Your bloodline is depending on you to adopt the spirit of forgiveness so that you can break the generational curses that plague your family. Unforgiveness will keep you in bondage to sickness and disease. Let's look at some of the symptoms and illnesses that unforgiveness causes.

There are many symptoms and sicknesses associated with unforgiveness, such as:

- High Blood Pressure
- Cancer
- Heart disease
- Depression
- Anxiety
- Paranoia
- Bitter
- Attention Seeking

- InsecureLow Self - Image.
- Plagued with negative thoughts
- Addictions (drugs, alcohol, food, and sex)
- Narcissism
- Controlling Behavior
- Timid
- Pushover
- Anger Issues
- Pride
- Hatred

    To heal from your past traumatic experiences, you must find it in your heart to forgive those who hurt you. First, you must make a conscious choice to forgive. Make up in your mind that you will not allow the pain from your past experiences to have control over your life any longer, release and let it go. In this next exercise, you will have the opportunity to just that.

FORGIVENESS EXERCISE

Earlier, you were instructed to leave the names of the people who hurt you taped to the wall. Go to the wall that you have their names taped to, and one by one, starting with the person closest to you (mother, father, family member, husband, etc.) and tell them why you forgive them. Or you can choose to write a letter to each of these people and burn them. Do this for everyone, all except yourself. (Your picture should remain taped to the mirror).

Remember that forgiveness is not a one-time event; it is a lifestyle. We live in a mean, cruel world, and there are going to be moments that you will face some pretty painful situations that will require you to forgive.

Athena Jackson

Forgiveness is not a sign of weakness but a sign of strength.

Congratulations, you just made a significant impact on your life! You awarded yourself the gift of forgiveness. Know that God is smiling and is pleased with your willingness to be set free so that you can be the person he created you to be. Your desire to forgive allows God to forgive you, and this will open a portal for breakthrough and blessings to rain in your life. Your best is yet to come, and you will witness it in the days ahead of you. God bless you as you embark on this new lifestyle of freedom.

THE GIFT OF FORGIVENESS

Prayer and Scriptures

Father, in the name of Jesus, I make a fresh commitment to You to live in peace and harmony, not only with the other brothers and sisters of the Body of Christ, but also with my friends, associates, neighbors, and family.

Father, I repent of holding on to bad feelings toward others. I bind myself to godly repentance and lose myself from bitterness, resentment, envying, strife, and unkindness in any form. Father, I ask Your forgiveness for my sins. By faith, I receive your forgiveness, having the assurance that I am clean from all unrighteousness through Jesus Christ. I ask You to forgive and release all who have wronged and hurt me. I forgive and release them.

Deal with them in your mercy and loving-kindness.

From this moment on, I purpose to walk in love, to seek peace, to live in agreement, and to conduct myself toward others in a manner that is pleasing to You. I know that I have right standing with You, and Your ears are attentive to my prayers.

Your word reveals that love has been poured forth into my heart by the Holy Ghost, who is given to me. I believe that love flows into the lives of everyone I know, that we may be filled with and abound in the fruits of righteousness, which bring glory and honor unto you, Lord, in Jesus' name. So be it! Amen.

Prayer from Prayers That Avail Much/To Walk in Forgiveness

Proverbs 17:9 (ESV) - Whoever would foster love covers over an offense, but whoever repeats the matter separates close friends.

Ephesians 4:32(ESV) - Be kind and compassionate to one another, forgiving each other, just as in Christ God forgave you

Colossians 3:13(ESV) - Bear with each other and forgive one another if any of you has a grievance against someone. Forgive as the Lord forgave you

Luke 6:37(ESV) - Do not judge, and you will not be judged. Do not condemn, and you will not be condemned. Forgive, and you will be forgiven.

Mark 11:25 (ESV)- And when you stand praying, if you hold anything against anyone, forgive them, so that your Father in heaven may forgive you your sins.

Athena Jackson

Soul Cleanse Day 7
THE PRISON SHAME

    Shame is a poison that eats away at our soul. Shame is formed from the wound of humiliation and is the emotional best friend to anger, bitterness, resentment, and humiliation. Addictions are formed when shame and guilt plague your mind. Shame will you to act out in more shameful ways.

    Most of my childhood and a great deal of my adulthood, I was shame ridden. I hung my head, filling guilty for what others had done to me. I was told by my sexual abusers when I was a 10 yr little girl he pursued me because of the way I walked or moved. I believed for years; it was my fault. I was ashamed. I tried to burry this toxic emotion but showed up in how I viewed myself and let others treat me. As life progressed, I made decisions that I was ashamed of and kept secret. These secrets and the toxic emotions tied to them were eating me alive.

Fear and shame are partners. When you are ashamed of something you want to hide that part of your life and fear sets in, you become scared for people to see you for who you are; therefore, the feelings of unworthiness and not being enough manifest and adds to your toxic emotions. Shame will cause you to isolate yourself, leaving you lonely and depressed. God did not design for you to live this way. It is ok not to be proud of the mistakes you made, but it is not ok to allow your mistakes to drag you to hell on earth.

Symptoms associated with shame:

- Fear of exposure and intimacy – being afraid of people finding out your past /who you truly.

- Plagued by feelings of not being enough, so you are driven by performance and being perfect

- Criticism devastates and disables you.

- Overly critical of other people

- People pleasers

- Being motivated and controlled by the opinions of other people.

- Being controlled by the fear of failure and rejection

- Underperforms and stays in a comfort zone to avoid the risk of being shamed
- Self-hatred – always belittling and beating yourself up.

    Condemnation and shame are Satan's trap to keep us separated from God's purpose.

God's will for us to live in authority; he warded us from the beginning. He proves this in genesis when he set Adam and Eve in the Garden of Eden and gave them full range over it and instructed them not to eat the fruit of the tree of knowledge. They were disobedient to God, and their guilt caused them to be humiliated., so they tried to hide from God with fig leaves. (Genesis 3:7-11) But God saw through the fig leaves. Although Adam and eve had to pay the price for their sins, he didn't want them to live a defeated life in condemnation. We have to remember that God's power is made perfect in our weakness. (2 Corinthians 12 8-10). God loves us despite our imperfections. Your fig leaves of shame do not hide your sins from God. He wants to remove your fig leaves of shame and all the attributes connected to it.

    To remove your fig leaves of shame, you must take responsibility, and trust God to forgive you. Until you take responsibility for your actions, you will continue to find scapegoats to hide. Adam tried to make Eve his scapegoat, and she did the same to the devil. Many people use their parents, spouses, jobs, and other people as their scapegoat throwing around blame. "It's my mother's fault; I'm the way I am." NO, and these people are not your problem, you are your problem. You have the choice of wearing the fig leaves or allowing yourself to become naked before God so He can heal your wounds.

"Confess your sins to God; he is a merciful and gracious God." (Psalms 103:8). When we confess our sins and repent, God forgets our sins. He will not throw it in your face nor plague you with thoughts of condemnation God showers you with love and wipes the slate clean. He allows you to begin again.

Just as God didn't want Adam and Eve to live in the bondage of shame, he doesn't want you to live in the bondage of shame. We are not perfect beings, we will make mistakes, and we do not have to punish ourselves by allowing the fear of embarrassment to keep us from our inner greatness. Shame causes us to focus on the wrong things. For a long time, shame held me in bondage to my comfort zone. The sad part, I didn't realize it was the shame that had me in bondage. I didn't know I was afraid to take risks because I feared to

Athena Jackson

expose my past mistakes and failures. My past was not different from most, I made mistakes just like everyone else, but the enemy amplified those mistakes, making me feel isolated. I was too afraid to leap.

    I was reflecting on the movie "The Lion King" and how Scar used guilt and shame to keep Simba from this rightful place as king. Scar amplified Simba's curiosity to see the site of dead bones to fault him for his father's death. Simba took complete responsibility for Mufasa's death and was shame ridden. Simba didn't know that Scar was responsible for his father's death, so he went and hid in shame. The enemy, like Scar, is deceitful, and he uses guilt to keep us from our inheritance. It is the enemy's job to attack you with the mistakes of your past. His goal is to make you feel like a failure so that you hang your head in shame. When he begins to attack your mind, immediately use your sword (the word of God) to defeat him. Romans 8:1-2 says, "Therefore, there is now no condemnation for those who are in Christ Jesus because through Christ Jesus the law of the Spirit who gives life has set you free from the law of sin and death." After you fight him with the word, thank God for the blood of Jesus that bore your sins on the cross and continue to move forward.

You've made mistakes like every other human on this earth. Ask God to forgive you, forgive yourself, and the people who hurt you then move forward. Ask God to help you embrace your uniqueness and stop hiding behind the scenes in fear of failure and exposure.

Athena Jackson

Stop trying to be perfect, because you will never be perfect. Know that you are enough and stand tall. You don't have to live in a prison of shame. God gave you a way out when he sent his son to die on the cross for us. He bore our guilt and shame on the cross. Shame pronounces us guilty and deficient. Jesus proclaims us guiltless and promises that his grace will be sufficient for us in all our weaknesses. The enemy wants us to live in the shackles of shame so that we can't fully experience God's love for us. Shame causes us to forfeit open doors and opportunities that will catapult us into our next level. Guilt and shame can be released through confession and processing the original painful experiences that caused it.

Self-Assessment.

Reflect on your shameful moments, include the ones in your childhood, and write them down.

_____
_____
_____
_____

_____

_____

Once you write them down, ask God for forgiveness. Ex. Father, forgive me for... Once you finish asking God for forgiveness then forgive yourself. I forgive myself for...

Shame leads to feelings of unworthiness and will cause you to settle for less than you deserve.

What areas in your life are you settling?

1. _____
_____
_____

2. _____
_____
_____

3. _____
_____
_____

Now put a plan in place to abandon your comfort zone. Example: If you are settling for a relationship where a person is frequently making you second guess yourself and makes you hang your head, its

Athena Jackson

time to clean house and let them go. Put a plan in place to leave this person because they mean you no good. As you leave, forgive them and pray that God brings them healing just as he did you.

THE PRISON OF SHAME

Prayer and Scripture

    I decree and declare that my past sins are inaccessible to Jesus, and me, He has removed them from me as far as the East is from the West. I decree and declare that I have nothing to fear because you don't give us the spirit of fear, and I will not be ashamed or disgraced any longer. I choose not to dwell on my past sins but will throw them into the sea of forgetfulness. I will not rehearse former reproachful life but will focus on the truth – that Christ has set me free from shame!

    I decree and declare that shame will no longer plague my life and that God will give me honor, and not just honor, but double honor, according to His promise!

Athena Jackson

    I renounce the hidden, shameful acts I have committed; they are now brought into light through my confession to Jesus and trusted leaders and friends. I am walking now in complete transparency, withholding nothing. I commend myself to anyone's conscience that I am cleansed and made whole.

    I decree and declare that there is therefore now no condemnation for me! I reject the thought that I am condemn-able, for Christ has made me acceptable to Himself!

    Father, as of this day, I will accept myself for myself, flaws, and all. I will shed my old garment of shame and humbly put on the garments of righteousness, purity, and praise.

    Whom the Son sets free is free indeed, so father today I rejoice as I walk in the freedom of shame and condemnation.

Father, thank you for opening my eyes and giving me awarding me second chances. I appreciate and pour my love on you in sincere gratitude.

In Jesus Name

Amen

Athena Jackson

1 Peter 2:6(ESV) - For it stands in Scripture: "Behold, I am laying in Zion a stone, a cornerstone chosen and precious, and whoever believes in him will not be put to shame."

John 10:10 (ESV)- The thief comes only to steal and kill and destroy. I came that they may have life and have it abundantly.

Isaiah 61:7 (ESV)- Instead of your shame there shall be a double portion; instead of dishonor they shall rejoice in their lot; therefore in their land, they shall possess a double portion; they shall have everlasting joy.

Hebrews 8:12 (ESV) - For I will be merciful toward their iniquities, and I will remember their sins no more."

Isaiah 54:4(ESV) - "Fear not, for you will not be ashamed; be not confounded, for you will not be disgraced; for you will forget the shame of your youth, and the reproach of your widowhood you will remember no more.

Soul Cleanse Day 8

SELF-FORGIVENESS

Releasing Blame, Shame, and Guilt

The past is in the past, and there is absolutely nothing that you can do about it. Your past mistakes, failures, should have, could have and would haves are over. You also can't rewind time and change the traumatic events that caused you pain. The people that hurt you cannot go back to change it, even if they wanted to. It's time to move on. Holding on the guilt of what you've done or didn't do and holding people hostage to what they did to you is not going to make your life any better, what's done is done and its over period. You are a strong individual who needs to reset your belief system so that you can walk in your purpose. It is now time to forgive yourself so that you can focus on your future.

God knew you would make mistakes when he created you. Your past actions were based on the damaged emotions that laid the foundations you or beliefs and actions at that time. From that moment to this one, no matter how long it was ago, you see things differently. Forgiving yourself is

Athena Jackson

most challenging because the toxic emotions help to build a wall of protection to prevent future hurt. When you release the blame, shame, and guilt from your past mistakes, you will then see life in a new light allowing you to live a more abundant, happier life without the burden of resentment.

    As you award yourself this liberating gift of self-forgiveness, you will also be releasing the sabotaging emotions that have you in bondage to your past. We will cover sabotaging emotions in tomorrow's lesson.

    When I forgave myself, it automatically opened a door for me to experience the peace and freedom I needed to conquer my fears and build my self-confidence. When I ceased throwing the blame game around, took ownership of my mistakes, and chose to be empathetic to the people who hurt me, a dark cloud lifted, and the skies became clear. Hurting people hurt people, so of course, there were people I hurt in my past. Just like I wanted forgiveness from the pain I caused, I had to learn be become empathetic so that I could forgive others as well as myself. I chose freedom over bondage and overtime, the demons of my past diminished and were able to embrace my purpose.

Self-Forgiveness Exercise

Your Name should still be hanging on your mirror. Head over to your mirror and say this:

"My sins were not only covered on the cross. But they are removed from me... taken so far from me and there is no way that they can be considered a part of me anymore. I understand that there is nothing to gain by holding myself hostage in the chains of unforgiveness and shame because there is everything to gain by releasing myself from shackles of unforgiveness and beginning the process of healing. Today I choose to move forward and make a positive difference in the future. I confess the ungodly accountability, a self-sabotaging mindset, and the vows I have made never to forgive myself. Because Jesus died for my sins, I choose to forgive myself, and I will no longer punish myself. I forgive myself for letting this hurt control me and for hurting others out of my pain. Today I am a new creature, and I choose to walk in my purpose free from the baggage of unforgiveness."

Now go in peace and enjoy your level of freedom!

Athena Jackson

SELF-FORGIVENESS

Prayer and Scriptures

Self-Forgiveness Prayer and Scripture are tied together in Psalms 51

Have mercy on me, O God, according to your unfailing love; according to your great compassion blot out my transgressions.

Wash away all my iniquity and cleanse me from my sin. For I know my transgressions, and my sin is always before me.

Against you, you only, have I sinned and done what is evil in your sight; so you are right in your verdict and justified when you judge.

Surely I was sinful at birth, sinful from the time my mother conceived me. Yet you desired faithfulness even in the womb; you taught me wisdom in that secret place. Cleanse me with hyssop, and I will be clean; wash me, and I will be whiter than snow.

Let me hear joy and gladness; let the bones you have crushed rejoice.

Hide your face from my sins and blot out all my iniquity.

Create in me a pure heart, O God, and renew a steadfast spirit within me.

Do not cast me from your presence or take your Holy Spirit from me.

Restore to me the joy of your salvation and grant me a willing spirit, to sustain me.

Then I will teach transgressors your ways so that sinners will turn back to you.

And my tongue will sing of your righteousness.

Open my lips, Lord, and my mouth will declare your praise.

You do not delight in sacrifice, or I would bring it; you do not take pleasure in burnt offerings.

God will not despise.

May it please you to prosper Zion, to build up the walls of Jerusalem.

Then you will delight in the sacrifices of the righteous, in burnt offerings offered whole; then bulls will be offered on your altar.

Soul Cleanse Day 9
ASKING FOR FORGIVENESS

Asking for forgiveness can be difficult and requires you to be humble. You are not perfect, and hurting people hurt people. As an individual who was emotionally damaged, it is likely you to have hurt other people. It works that way, but it doesn't mean you don't owe someone an apology.

In my healing process, I owed some people an apology. I've hurt people out of my hurt, even my children. My children saw me being mistreated and saw how I allowed other people to overstep boundaries, as a matter of fact, I didn't have very many. They resented me for that. They saw me compromise my self-worth the be accepted, along with a host of actions that people who suffer need healing do. I owed them an apology and sat them down one by one and gave it to them. Somewhere open, some took more time. It was ok because it freed me, and over time it freed them.

You may owe a few people an apology, and it's ok. Today I am going to challenge you to another exercise. Below I need you to write down the name of the people you've hurt due to your damaged emotions, including your children. (if your children saw you mistreat someone or saw you mistreated, they were hurt because of someone you brought into the home, you abused, cursed them, abandoned, neglected, or shut them out write their names down)

1. _____

2. _____

3. _____

4. _____

5. _____

Now for each name you wrote down, one by one ask each these people for forgiveness. God has already forgiven you, and you have forgiven yourself for your past mistakes. It is now time for you to make peace with the people who you've hurt. Forgiveness will not only help them, but it will free you. If a person is not willing to talk, send them a letter but use this method only If they refuse to talk. Be brave; this is a vital part of your healing process. So what if the person is not willing to forgive you?

This may very well be the case, but don't take it personally, they too need to heal, and one day you may look up and see that they have forgiven you. Your humbleness in asking forgiveness may be the very thing they need to start their healing process.

ASKING FOR FORGIVENESS

Prayer and Scripture

Today is your turn to write your prayer, use the space below to talk to god. Say whatever you need to say, there is no right or wrong way to speak to him; he is listening to your heart as you write.

Father in the name of Jesus,

_____
_____
_____
_____
_____
_____
_____
_____
_____
_____
_____
_____

Athena Jackson

_____
_____
_____
_____
_____
_____
_____
_____
_____
_____
_____
_____
_____

_____

In Jesus name, Amen

Soul Cleanse Day 10
DETOX YOUR RELATIONSHIPS

Relationships play an imperative role in our lives, yet they can be one of the most toxic aspects of our lives. Relationships that generate toxic emotions such as fear, insecurity, anxiety, jealousy, hatred, and depression are of no use to us. These contaminated emotions manifest in our bodies, and until we detox them, it doesn't matter how many health supplements you take, how much you exercise, Toxic relationships have adverse effects on your health.

On your healing journey, you will come to terms with the fact that you have to release people. These people can be your significant others, associates, friends, even family members. Toxic people will hinder your healing process, so you must separate yourself from these individuals. Healthy relationships foster healthy emotions; they encourage growth and happiness.

Here are a few steps to detox your relationships:

First, you must understand that you attract who you are. These toxic relationships reflect something going on within yourself; unhealed individuals attract unhealed individuals. When you begin to accept the fact that you are a fantastic individual who deserves to be respected and loved, you will not settle for anyone who brings anything less to the table. You will eat alone before you eat with anyone who is dishing out toxic behavior.

The secret is knowing your worth. When you don't know who you are, you are open for anyone to tell you who you are. Seasoned toxic people prey on weaker toxic people; they seek them out, so they don't have to deal with the issues of their hearts and spew their venom, causing these individuals to become more toxic. When you know your worth, you repel these toxic individuals.

The secret to knowing your worth is getting to know your creator. How will you know your worth if you don't know who your creator is? The reason why many people struggle with knowing their worth is that they don't know who God is. What does God say about you? What are his plans for you? Understand that God knows all of your past mistakes and failures. He looks past the people who left you and caused you to suffer from the root of rejection and have abandonment issues or whatever emotional trauma you suffered from. God sees you for who you are, so rest in the fact that you are valuable to him no matter what. The only way to know how valuable you are to God is to spend time with him.

Affirm yourself daily; every day, speak over your life. What you rehearse in your conscious mind will eventually settle in your subconscious mind, and you will become the affirmations you speak, and you will begin to attract these attributes in other people.

Make a list of the people you are in contact with most often, and beside each person's name, write the emotions associated with that person. While you may love or care for some of these individuals, write down if they make you second guess yourself, do you feel drained after spending time with them, are you angry when you are around them? Do they make you feel insecure? Are they negative? Also, write if they make you feel inspired, encouraged, enlightened, or happy. Be

Athena Jackson

honest with yourself, and for those that trigger those negative emotions, it may be time to cut the cord to those relationships.

Toxic relationships can serve as security blankets until we began to heal, but the longer you hold on these relationships, the longer it takes to heal. Toxic people have a way of reminding us of our past and speaking to our "I'm not enough" during our healing process. Yes, this is challenging, yet it is vital. You are making room for those healthy relationships to spring up as you cut out the toxic ones.

There is no easy way to let go of toxic relationships. I found it easier to create distance between the toxic people in my life and me, especially family. I became less available for events and started doing new things. You can do the same thing. Try new hobbies; if you are not involved in your community, now is a great time to become involved. Take some classes that you've always wanted to take, fill your time with new things, and you will not only name room for new healthy relationships, but you will disconnect from the old toxic ones.

Soul Cleanse Day 11
RELINQUISHING BITTER ROOT JUDGEMENTS

What are bitter root judgements?

A root is a source lying under the surface; it is the fuel and nutrition the element on surface. Root doesn't surface, but it feeds the surface Bitter Root Judgments are inner vows that you promised yourself you would do or never do. These vows are usually made as children and are a form of bitterness.

An example of Bitter Root Judgment:

Your mother had a boyfriend/husband who was not your biological father, and he punished you. You make a vow to never have another man outside of your children's father over your children,

Or let's say your father was an alcoholic, and you vowed to never date an alcoholic because of the pain caused by your father's alcoholism.

These are examples of bitter root judgment. These vows stem from the unresolved issues and

Athena Jackson

developed into unforgiveness/bitterness, and this caused you to judge. Unfortunately, bitter root judgments have a way backfiring in your life. When I was young, I vowed never to date a drunk. Now that I looked back the men, I dated had a drinking problem. It wasn't until I was educated on bitter root judgments that I made the connection. When we make those vowels, we are essentially passing judgment on people. The only way to relinquish those judgments is through forgiveness. Although we covered unforgiveness, we can still hold on to judgments unknowingly. Today you are going to uncover the inner vows you made.

You must release these judgments so you can break the cycle. The buck stops here.

In this exercise write down some of the vows you made from anger and bitterness.

1._____
_____

2._____
_____

3._____
_____

4._____
_____

Athena Jackson

Once I was able to Identify my bitterroot judgments, I was able to release them. I was angry with my father for years, and because I was so resentful, he continued to show up in the men I chose. The time came when I offered some empathy towards my father. He was not born a drunk, and I'm pretty sure this was not how he vision his life would be. He had unresolved issues, and he refused to let his past go. He was a hurting man who needed to forgive. Because he chose to hold on to his pain, he turned to alcohol to numb it. It wasn't personal. He loved me, he loved all his children, but all of us were affected by his choice to hold on to unforgiveness. Hurting people hurt people, and when I came to terms with that, my feelings towards him changed.

My father did not deserve me to forgive him, but just as God had mercy and understood the mistakes I made, I offered the same compassion to my father. Forgiveness helped me to release that bitter root judgment, and a burden was lifted.

Take a moment and put your feet in your offender's shoes; this will allow you to see them in a different light. Take your feelings out of the situation and see it for what it was and offer empathy. Taking this step will allow you to release the inner vowels and judgment.

RELINQUISHING BITTER ROOT JUDGMENT

Prayer and Scriptures

Father in the name of Jesus,

I come before you asking your forgiveness for the bitterness I have carried in my heart. I have stored my hurts on the shelves of my heart, avoiding the pain of my past. I have made judgments against people who caused me to be emotionally damaged. As of this day, I choose to let it go. Father root out any bitterness, iniquity, and any other spirit that does not align with your word. Create in me a clean heart and renew in me a right spirit. I am no longer running and pretending like I'm whole and ok. My heart has been broken, it has endured a lot, but I trust and release this pain unto you. I am open for you to pour into me your wisdom, knowledge, and understanding as you heal my damaged emotions. I cast down every wicked imagination and limiting beliefs the try and plague my mind. I renounce my old mindset as I

Athena Jackson

adopt this new mind of Christ. Thank you for new beginnings in Jesus name, Amen

Matthew 6:34 (ESV)- "Therefore, do not be anxious about tomorrow, for tomorrow will be anxious for itself. Sufficient for the day is its own trouble.

Isaiah 41:10 (ESV)- Fear not, for I am with you; be not dismayed, for I am your God; I will strengthen you, I will help you, I will uphold you with my righteous right hand.

Jeremiah 17:7-8(ESV) - "Blessed is the man who trusts in the Lord, whose trust is the Lord. He is like a tree planted by water, that sends out its roots by the stream, and does not fear when heat comes, for its leaves remain green, and is not anxious in the year of drought, for it does not cease to bear fruit."

Athena Jackson

Soul Cleanse Day 12
OVERCOMING SELF-DEFEAT

    Have you ever decided to do something like start college, lose weight, apply for a new position or start a business, just to be haunted by thoughts like," what if I fail," I'm not qualified enough," no one will support my business." After giving in to those self-sabotaging thoughts, you just quit, and later on, you beat yourself up for not moving forward.

    Your past experiences shape your inner voice. It is made up of your parents, your teachers, siblings, community, along with the influences that contribute to our belief system. If your parents called you stupid, you tend to believe that you're not capable of making the right decisions. Or maybe your parents called you lazy, and you adopted the belief that you were useless. Say your parents constantly compared you to other people, and now you are extremely competitive, always looking to outdo other people, or you settle for less because you don't feel worthy enough to have the best.

Romans 7:24 Chapter 8 is the answer

The problem with me is me. I am my worst enemy

Seven weapons of the mind that contribute to Self-defeat

- 1st weapon - self-destruction is shame
- 2nd weapon - uncontrolled thoughts
- 3rd weapon - compulsion - I just had to do it. You can lose an entire life in compulsion
- 4th weapon - fear
- 5th Hopelessness -nothing to live for.
- 6th Bitterness – It is a self-destructive emotion, and it will eat you alive
- 7th insecurity – Not being enough

My mother showed us an abundance of love and told us a few times a day how much she loved us. She was also a fuss box and yelled often. I also attended a church that gave me a great foundation and taught me the word of God but often reminded us how God doesn't like when we sinned, and hell awaits a sinner so that I would beat myself

Athena Jackson

up for my mistakes. Our mistakes were often put on front street, and we were sometimes humiliated. In my perception, the church was fear-driven 'You will go to hell for your sins, and the saints were judgmental" as opposed to God loves you, and we show our gratitude towards him by living according to his word and when you sin, repent and sin no more.

I grew up allowing my inner critic to yell at me, repetitively beating myself up for small mistakes telling myself I didn't deserve this or that because of my mistakes. This self-sabotaging behavior was cultivated in me as a child. I was a product of my environment. Neither my mother nor my church meant any harm, but their tactics were, unknowingly to them, were counter-productive. Being sexually abused by family members and close family friends contributed to my belief that I wasn't worthy of love, and my voice was not important. I often allowed people to overstep their boundaries.

Neglecting to set healthy boundaries only made my inner critic to scream louder, with thoughts like "your stupid," your weak," "you are unloved and unappreciated." These thoughts led to some of the following self-sabotaging habits.

- Speaking meanly to myself
- Thinking mean thoughts about others
- Staying up late when I'm tired
- Procrastination
- Abandonment
- Unhealthy eating
- Unhealthy relationships
- Bad spending habits
- Yoyo dieting/ binge eating
- Talking myself out of commitments

These bad habits strengthened my emotions of resentment, guilt, and shame. It wasn't until I started down my journey to healing, did I realize why I procrastinated when it was time for me to

Athena Jackson

take on or complete challenging tasks. My fear of failure and belief of not being enough caused me to abandon the critical task, my health, my relationships, and other essential things. Once I got to the root of why I would sabotage my process, I attacked my belief system. Forgiving the people who hurt me was just the beginning, but I read books, listen to various pastors, attended healing conferences, and incorporated daily positive affirmations. Over time my belief system started to change, and when my belief system changed, so did those self-sabotaging habits.

7 Habits to break the cycle of self-defeat:

1st step - Remind yourself that whom the Son sets free is free indeed (St John 8:36) You are an overcomer. Ask God to expose your defeated mindset behind your cycle of defeat. People work on outside behavior, but they don't work on the mindset that produces the action. Release any feelings of bitterness, resentment, and unforgiveness, shame is a sin. When you submit those sins to the cross, change begins — the battle to be free starts in mind. If I am acting depressed, it's because I'm feeling depressed and focusing on the past, and if I'm feeling sad, I'm thinking depressing thoughts. (Whatsoever a man thinketh in his heart so is he) When you change the way you think, it will change the way you feel, and it will change the way you.

2nd Mental habit. - Ask the holy spirit to give you better thoughts. During a storm, you can either accept defeat, or you ask the holy spirit to give you peace. You can rely on god's word, or you can lean to our own understanding. When you want to break a bad habit, you don't want to resist it, but refocus. So instead of focusing on who left you, shift your focus on who loves you. The devil's ideas are tempting; the holy spirits ideas are inspiring **(Roman 8:7-8)**

Athena Jackson

3rd Mental Habit - I can say no. God has given us the power to say " NO" God has empowered us with the holy spirit who is our helper, and when we allow the holy spirit to live and operate in me, I can resist the enemy, and he will flee. Just because I am a believer doesn't mean I'm not going to have desires, but God has given me the power to resist the enemy. The bible says our heart is desperately wicked, but he also has the power to create in us a clean heart. **(Romans 8:9 -12)**

4th Mental habit - Seek Gods when you are afraid **(Romans 8:14-16**) stop focusing on your fear, focus on your father. Focus on the promises of God. Remember that you belong to God, and he is your protector; he is your father; he is your healer. **2nd Timothy 1:7** God has not given us the spirit of fear.

5th Mental Habit - Focus on the long term, not the short term. The longer-term your thinking is, the more successful you will be in life. The shorter-term you think, the less successful you will be. When you believe in the long term, you can handle short term pain more effectively. What does your life look like in 10 years? What do you have to sacrifice today to become achieve that 10 hears gold? **Roman 8: 17-18**

6th mental habit: Everyday, remember how good God is good to you. Have a spirit of gratitude. Take the time to thank God for who he is, for the small things in your life. Your house, your shoes, the food you eat, your family, the sun, the moon, and the stars. Whatever you can think of, stop, and give God thanks each day. Life is going to happen, the pain will occur, storms will come, but you don't have to be miserable. Bitterness comes when we allow pain to change our thoughts toward God. **(Romans 8:28)** Know that God created you to prosper, be in good health even as your soul prospers, so he will always provide.

7th mental habit: Know that you are enough. Insecurities will make us feel like we are not worthy of love. Insecurity is birthed out of rejection, and rejection hurts. God doesn't reject you, he made you, and he doesn't make anything without meaning or purpose.

Develop a daily routine with the intention to win. Plant seeds for your future and set your life up to win by consistently giving showing up one hundred percent to your dreams. Don't allow social

Athena Jackson

media and other media to make you compare yourself to other people. Remember that you are enough.

You have within yourself to change your belief system. This next exercise is designed to help you identify your limiting beliefs and where they originated. You will also learn how to identify the habits that were formed from your limiting beliefs.

Self-Assessment:

It is your turn to identify the root of your belief system. Take a few mins and reflect on your childhood and or the events that helped shape your self-sabotaging belief system. Write down the event that shaped the belief, then write down the belief system that was formed from that event.

1.
_____

2.
_____

3.
_____

Athena Jackson

Write down the self-sabotaging habits that you created as a result of your belief system

Ex. Unhealthy Eating

1._____

2._____

3.
_____

4._____

5._____

6._____

For the next seven days, be extra mindful of your thoughts, take note of the self any self-sabotaging thoughts and behaviors, and write them down. Also, write down the event triggered those thoughts and actions.

Example:

You start binge eating, stop, and write down the thoughts or the events that are causing you to binge.

SELF-DEFEAT

Prayer and Scriptures

    Father, in the name of Jesus, I ask you to forgive me too for not standing on your word concerning my life. You said I am more than a conquer through him that loves us, and I can do all things through Christ who strengthens me. Today at this moment, I choose to believe in who you called me to be. Father, I ask you to heal my inner parts and root out any shame, guilt, resentment, vengeful, self-sabotaging thoughts that cause me to miss out on the plans you have for me. I renounce any habit I formed as a result of my old sabotaging belief system. As you forgive me, I too forgive myself for neglecting to cast down wicked imaginations. Father, as I complete my journey of inner healing, I invite the holy spirit to lead and guide me. I give you access to my mind, my will, and my emotions. In Jesus name…amen

Romans 12:2(ESV) - Do not be conformed to this world, but be transformed by the renewal of your mind, that by testing you may discern what is the will of God, what is good and acceptable and perfect.

1 John 3:20-21(ESV) -For whenever our heart condemns us, God is greater than our heart, and he knows everything. Beloved, if our heart does not condemn us, we have confidence before God;

Proverbs 28:26(ESV) - Whoever trusts in his own mind is a fool, but he who walks in wisdom will be delivered

Psalm 139:13-14(ESV) - For you formed my inward parts; you knitted me together in my mother's womb. I praise you, for I am fearfully and wonderfully made. Wonderful are your works; my soul knows it very well.

Soul Cleanse Day 13

HEALING ADDICTIONS

The Greek word most often translated "overcomer" stems from the word *Nike* which, according to *Strong's Concordance*, means "to carry off the victory."

Overcoming any addiction can be super challenging, whether it is alcohol, drugs, food, sex, or even a toxic relationship. No matter how challenging it may be, remember you more than a conquer through him that loves you, and this battle is already won. Christ bore all our afflictions on the cross, so understand that you are healed. All you need to do is walk in it. Though this is not a comfortable journey, it's a victorious one. 1 Corinthians 10:13 says (ESV), "No temptation has overtaken you that is not common to man. God is faithful, and he will not let you be tempted beyond your ability, but with the temptation, he will also provide the way of escape, that you may be able to endure it." So, you see, God has already made a way of escape.

During your healing process, you must become your number one priority. Take some time for yourself, join a support group. If you're not already a member of a church, it is a good idea to join and connect with a spiritual leader. Also, hire a good coach or go to counseling. Heal on purpose is a great start but will need to continue your healing process with other resources.

Don't play the blame game; however, you got to this point no longer matters. You are on a new victorious journey, and you are no longer tied to your history. Disconnect from toxic people who want to remind you of all of your mistakes; you have to let them go, yes, even if they are family. Identify toxic relationships and let them go.

Be patient with yourself. You didn't become an addict overnight and won't conquer this overnight, but you will overcome it. You will have good days, and you will have bad days. Don't beat yourself up; just keep going. Your support system is important, share your struggle with them and allow them to encourage you. Don't let shame and guilt to eat at you if you slip up, forgive yourself a move on the understanding that you are human and will make mistakes. Don't use your mistakes as a reason to keep slipping; you are in this to win through all of your excuses out of the window. You are now a champion!

A few additional steps in winning the victory over addictions:

Athena Jackson

Put a plan in place to win this battle. Start by finding a local support group that deals with your addiction, if you belong to a church contact your spiritual leader and let them know you are ready to deal with your addiction so they can support you. Some addictions require an overnight stay, prepare for that. Let your family and employer know the steps you are taking so they can be prepared.

Let your family know that you are setting out heal. If you go to bars on certain days, replace it with another productive activity or hobbies. Join a gym if you're not already a member or get in a routine of walking. Many people who overcome addictions, do it by adding a great exercise regimen to their daily routine.

Spend time with God daily. Cast your cares on him, you can trust him, and he will never fail you as you spend time with him in prayer and reading his word. He will begin to reveal his plan for your life. Even if you know what it is you are called to do, he will give you a better vision of yourself.

The secret to overcoming any addiction is by building your relationships with God.

When your flesh gets weak, he will renew your strength; there nothing God can't handle.

Bring your thoughts and words in alignment with Gods word. 2 Corinthians 10:5 says " *Casting down imaginations, and every high thing that exalteth itself against the knowledge of God, and bringing into captivity every thought to the obedience of Christ; "The* victory over addictions start in your mind, so irrigate negative thoughts at the point of entrance. As negative thoughts start in, cast them down immediately. It was the rehearsal of old negative thought patterns that paved the way for you to become an addict, and it will be the rehearsal of God's word the will free you from that addiction.

   Proverbs 18:21 tells us that " Death and life are in the power of the tongue, and they that love it shall eat the fruit thereof." Your words have power, so watch what you say. The devil can't read your mind, but he can hear your words and will use them against you. Guard your words and use your mouth to speak life. You are an overcomer, so say it, you are more than a conquer, so say it, the shackles of your past no longer bind you, you are forgiven, and you are free. Say those things. Our words have a way of showing up in our lives, so say words you want to manifest in your life.

Beware of toxic conversations, whether it's about you or someone else. If sally is sleeping with Johnny, that is sally and Johnny's problem, not yours. Other people's opinions of you are none of your business. Make that clear to the who want to fill you full of their venom. The enemy is looking for a way to keep you bound. He will use anything and anyone to do it. 1st Peter 5:8 says to "Be sober, be vigilant; because of your adversary the devil, as a roaring lion, walketh about, seeking whom he may devour:"

Secrets will keep you feeling guilty and shameful. Expose the enemy and allow your spiritual leaders, a trusted family member, or counselor to know what's been eating at you. Your not the first to make the mistakes you made, and you won't be the last. Shed light on the darkness you've been living in and watch your life began to change. Don't allow pride to keep you in bondage; let it go!

You are an overcomer

Overcomers are followers of Christ who successfully resist the power and temptation of the world's system. An overcomer is not sinless, but they hold fast to faith in Christ until the end. He does not turn away when times get difficult or become an apostate. Overcoming requires complete dependence upon God for direction,

purpose, fulfillment, and strength to follow His plan for our lives. Overcomers are promised a great reward, and they will eat from the Tree of Life. (Revelations 2:7) Choosing to overcome your addictions and toxic thinking patterns has benefits. God rewards you for choosing to trust in his word. God does not hold your addictions nor the sins you committed against you once you confess your sins and trust him with your past. **When you bring your hidden sins into the light, God will deliver you. Your past mistakes will become a steppingstone to your victorious future. God has a way of using our past in our favor.** Jerimiah 29:11 says
For I know the thoughts that **I** think toward you, saith the Lord, thoughts of peace, and not of evil, to give you an expected end.

Athena Jackson

Overcoming Addictions

Prayer and Scriptures

Father, in the name of Jesus

I ask your forgiveness for not trusting you with my emotional pain. Father, I am asking you to heal my wounded soul and the addictions formed from those wounds. I decree and declare that I am no longer a slave to my addictions. Father, I ask you to demolish the satisfaction, pleasure, and comfort that my addictive behavior. Purge me and destroy the grip that addiction it has on my life. Father grace me as I learn to turn to your word for comfort and strength. Give me the strength to deal with the confusion and pain that addiction caused in my life and my family's life. Father, I ask you to heal my feelings of shame and humiliation as I recover from my addiction. Heal the wounds that my addiction may have caused the people that I love. Father, I ask you to create in me a clean heart and renew in me a right spirit. Wash me white as snow.

Father, I speak a peace that passes all understanding over my mind. I command my mind will and emotions to come in line with your purpose for my life. Father, thank you for this chance to repent and turn from bad habits and self-sabotaging behaviors that interrupt your will for my life. Thank you, father, for sending your only begotten son to die on the cross so that I may be set free from the bondage of sin. I appreciate the love you have for me; thank you for your grace and mercy. In Jesus name, Amen

Psalms 107:19-20 (ESV) - Then they cried to the Lord in their trouble, and he saved them from their distress. He sent out his word and healed them; he rescued them from the grave.

Jeremiah 17:14 (ESV) - Heal me, Lord, and I will be healed; save me and I will be saved, for you are the one I praise."

Matthew 11:28-30(ESV) - Come to me, all you who are weary and burdened, and I will give you rest. Take my yoke upon you and learn from me, for I am gentle and humble in heart, and you will find rest for your souls. For my yoke is easy and my burden is light.

Athena Jackson

James 5:15-16 (ESV)- And the prayer offered in faith will make the sick person well; the Lord will raise them up. If they have sinned, they will be forgiven. Therefore, confess your sins to each other and pray for each other so that you may be healed. The prayer of a righteous person is powerful and effective

NO MATTER THE SITUATION, NEVER LET YOUR emotions OVERPOWER Your intelligence.

Emotional Detox Day 14

HEALING EMOTIONAL DEPENDENCY

Fear is the foundation of emotional dependency (co-dependency). This fear has people wasting years in unhealthy, unproductive relationships. It is the reason people stay stuck in situations that no longer serve them. Emotional dependency will keep you from experiencing true happiness. When you are not confident in who you are and what your purpose is, you give fear permission to have total access, and it rules your life. Breaking free from the bondage of fear requires you to change your mind about who you believe you are and who you think you are not. Fear forms emotional filters that block your ability to embrace authentic self; therefore, you lack the confidence to leave your comfort zone and run the risk of being controlled and manipulated, craving validation from outside sources.

Fear is a terrible emotion that paralyzes us and keeping us from experiencing true happiness. Fear is designed to keep us in bondage to our limiting beliefs. Some of the fears that are holding people for becoming the person they were created to be:

Athena Jackson

Fear of rejection and criticism

Fear of the loss of love (abandonment)

Fear of embarrassment and ridicule. (Humiliation and shame)

Fear the loss of respect or esteem of others.

Fear of the loss of their jobs and financial security.

     These fears have robbed people of their destiny for years. The graveyard is filled with people who were creative and talented, people who had mass potential, but they allowed fear to dominate their minds and died before they were able to release their inner champions. Don't let fear rob you of your happiness, not one more minute. Make a choice to deal with those fearful thoughts by identifying where they come from. What life event caused you to fear to be alone? What dreadful event caused you to be second guess your worth? When I realized that my father leaving our family had nothing to do with me, or that me being molested didn't mean I was worthless or the people who labeled me and put me in a box didn't mean I had to dummy down my intelligence to make them right. I learned to conquer my fears by addressing them head-on and disconnecting from the negative emotions tied to them.

I Healed on Purpose

Athena Jackson

    Write down the past events that formed your fears of being alone and then disconnect from the negative emotions tied to them. You have the power over your fears; they do not have to consume you. Face your fears of being alone by embracing your alone time and healing the wounds of your past. Embrace your fear of rejection by doing that one small thing you continue to put off in fear of ridicule. Just do it. When you force yourself to face your fears, your self-esteem builds, your self-respect increases, and your sense of personal pride grows.

    You don't need to be validated, and you are a powerhouse by yourself. Most people don't want to be alone, but when you are emotionally dependent on other people, those people have the power to control your happiness. Take your power back by healing your need to be validated and your fears of being alone. Your inner champion is ready to be unleashed so you can fulfill your purpose.

I'm not
here to be
average.
I'm here
to be
AWESOME

Athena Jackson

Emotional Detox Day 14

HEALING THE WOUNDS OF FORNICATION

Every time you have sexual intercourse with someone, you become one flesh with that person. An unhealthy soul tie is then formed because you are united to that person in every way possible. Soul ties formed from sex outside of marriage causes a person to become defiled:

Fornication produces short-term pleasure, but the consequences are long -term sorrow. It is an unclean demonic spirit that gets legal access through fornication. This demonic unclean spirit uses of fornication as their ticket to enter. This legal access causes the person to become more entangled in the sin of fornication, making it harder for them to stop fornication.

Fornication can start as entertainment of the mind that eventually thought moves into the realm of the heart where it becomes a consuming passion. This affection of the heart destroys our relationship with the Lord because our hearts are filled with other things, which are not pleasing to God. Our hearts are far from Him.

Fornication is not what it appears to be. You are literally playing with fire when and are entertaining demonic spirits. It is an open door for the enemy to have a field day in your soul. Fornication is not an innocent act. It might appear to be fun and exciting, but it comes with heavy baggage. It is the devil's way of keeping us separated from God.

However, there is hope. God always provides a way of escape from temptation. If you know you struggle in this area, be mindful of putting yourself in situations that leave you vulnerable and open to acting on that temptation (i.e., late-night visits to 'chill' and watch a movie, flirtatious texting).

If you are in a relationship and you truly love your mate - love them enough to commit to waiting until you're ready to enter a covenant of marriage and become their lifelong mate.

Athena Jackson

Consequences of Fornication

- *Shame*
- *Guilt*
- *Disappointment*
- *Feelings of Rejection, humiliation, betray, and betrayal.*

Abortion - Abortion came about as a result of man trying to cover up sin. Due to disobedience to God, approximately 46 million babies have been aborted since 1973.

Dysfunctional families - Due to fornication, 40 percent of babies are born out of marriage yearly. Fornication also relates to why 50% of marriages end in divorce. This is because many enter into marriage with wounded emotions.

Sickness and Diseases - 100,000 to 150,000 women become infertile each year as a result of STDs.

1 Corinthians 6:12-20 says:

12. *All things are lawful for me, but all things are not helpful. All things are lawful for me, but I will not be brought under the power of any.*

13. Foods for the stomach and the stomach for foods, but God will destroy both it and them. Now the body is not for sexual immorality but for the Lord, and the Lord for the body.

14. And God both raised up the Lord and will also raise us up by His power.

15. Do you not know that your bodies are members of Christ? Shall I then take the members of Christ and make them members of a harlot? Certainly not!

16. Or do you not know that he who is joined to a harlot is one body with her? For "The two," He says, "shall become one flesh."

17. But he who is joined to the Lord is one spirit with Him.

18. Flee sexual immorality. Every sin that a man does is outside the body, but he who commits sexual immorality sins against his own body.

19. Or do you not know that your body is the temple of the Holy Spirit who is in you, whom you have from God, and you are not your own?

20. For you were bought at a price; therefore, glorify God in your body and in your spirit, which are God's.

Athena Jackson

These scriptures allow us to understand that sexual intercourse is a communion of life. Your spirit, emotions, every aspect of your being is all becomes one with that person. You become joined to the person or people you have sex with. The word " joined" in the Greek means "glued to" when you have sex outside of marriage, you become joined (glued) to them, therefore sex is made for the marital bed. In a godly marriage, God links the two together, and the Bible tells us that they become one flesh. As a result of them becoming one flesh, it binds them together, and they will uniquely cleave onto one another. The purpose of this cleaving is to build a very healthy, strong, and close relationship between a man and a woman.

When you pull apart something that is glued together, there is always damage to one or both parts, and sometimes it is excruciating to disconnect the parts. This can create intense emotional trauma Sometimes, when there is a separation of something glued together, a portion of one of the pieces may remain attached even when the two parts have separated. This happens for everyone you had sexual relations with, whether you were married or not.

Some indicators that you have ungodly soul ties from sexual immorality include:

- Tormented by thoughts about a person.
- You are excessively wondering about them, checking on them, and rehearsing times with them.

Other ways unhealthy soul ties are formed:

- Toxic, unhealthy, abusive relationships (physically, sexually, emotionally, verbally)
- Adultery
- Premarital sex - fornication
- Obsessive entanglements with a person (giving them more authority in your life than you give to God)
- Controlling relationships

If you've confessed and repented of the sin of fornication, then God has washed it away. You are forgiven, and God has forgotten about it. 1 John 1:9 says that *"If we confess our sins, He is faithful and just to forgive us our sins and to cleanse us from all unrighteousness."*

      Belittling, shaming, and guilt-feelings are how the enemy keeps us from reuniting with our creator. These feelings of condemnation are not from God. Our father does not condemn us; he is waiting on you to repent so that he can create in you a clean heart and wash you from your sins. God loves you, and he is not ashamed of you. Romans 8: 1-12 tells us *"There is therefore now no condemnation to them which are in Christ Jesus, who walk not after the flesh, but after the Spirit. 2 For the law of the Spirit of life in Christ Jesus hath made me free from the law of sin and death."*

SPIRITUAL BOOT CAMP

A boot camp is a short rigorous course of training. This next segment is designed to empower you to conquer your fears so that you can give birth to the champion that is inside of you. You will learn to overcome a defeated mindset. For years you've allowed your perception and damaged emotions to influence your decision making. This spiritual boot camp is going to help you to experience life at a new level.

If you are ready to walk in your purpose, you must have a healthy relationship with your creator. It is he who knows why he put you on this earth, and it is through him that you will fulfill your purpose. God has a unique secret ingredient in your life. He has your answers, not your past, not other people's opinions of you, not even your parents, but God does. He wants to reveal them to you; he wants to show you to you.

Now that you have emptied it's time to download what you need to live like the champion, you were created to be by adopting the mindset of a conqueror. You've endured some major storms, and this has placed you in the runner up to be a champion — all you need in the tools and weapons to catapult you to the next level. The secret to

Athena Jackson

unlocking your inner power is in the word of God. It is in his word that you will get the weapons you need to defeat the giants that hinder your growth and keep you stagnant.

You were born a champion with the wings of an eagle, and you will learn to become comfortable soaring among the stars. The average is no acceptable, nor will you tolerate it. You will develop your wings as you get to know your creator and understand your purpose. To understand your purpose, it's a must that you know who God is. Once you know who he is, you will gain a better understanding of who you are and your ability to achieve your dreams.

When you read and get an understanding of God's word, you gain the confidence necessary to spread your wings and fly and therefore take your rightful place the starts. Your days of settling for a chicken mentality are over. You are not assigned to the ground; your rightful place is in the sky among the other eagles. The difference between you and the eagles who are currently soaring is your mindset. If you change your mind, you change your destiny.

God has privileged us, in Christ Jesus, to live above the "Ordinary" human plane of life. We are the head and not the tail, above and not beneath!

Spiritual Boot Camp

Day 1

A WINNING BELIEF SYSTEM

Daily our minds are constantly bombarded with information from various outside sources such as social media and television that disturbs and can disrupt our spiritual growth. Paul reminds us that our bodies are living sacrifices, and our thoughts should not be confirmed or influenced by the ways of this world. It is essential to filter out any information that does not align with the word of God. This is why we must read God's word daily so that when the cares of this world try to overtake our minds, we have a defense mechanism in place to repel anything that will defile our inner man and cause us to revert to our old way of thinking.

Think about a time when you allowed your emotions to get the best of you, just to be plagued with feelings of regret, shame, resentment, and guilt afterward. Excitement and pain are among our universal emotions. We are driven daily by our feelings; they regulate our thoughts and actions, sometimes reign superior over our rational minds.

Unmanaged, damaged emotions created from a limited belief, will consistently lead to negative results. We can't always control how we feel, but we can monitor how we are responding our emotions. Operating in a healthy belief system means allowing the word of God to take precedence over your emotions. The word of God tells us we are more than conquers, so when fear arises, respond with facts from the word of God as opposed to responding to your emotions. Make it a habit to combat your negative thoughts with positive ones. When you conquer your limiting beliefs by transforming your mind, your quality of life will change, and you will be liberated. A Healthy belief system offers us the freedom to explore our authentic selves.

If you don't make a habit of operating in your new belief system, you will quickly fall back into your limiting beliefs. You also have to be mindful of the old emotional patterns as they arise. For example; As I began to heal, instead of picking up the phone seeking approval, I got a mentor to and began to seek direction. I would also choose relationships where I could play hero because I didn't think I was good enough for anyone who knew their worth. Playing the hero would give me a temporary high that I was in some way worthy.

Athena Jackson

You have power over your emotions, and the more you choose to operate out of your head instead of your emotions, your life will change. When people attack your character with lies, such as you're not qualified enough, know that favor is upon you, and God has the last say. When people disappoint you, don't take it personally. When you fail at something, learn the lesson from it and get up and start over but don't beat up on yourself for trying. Champions fail at things; failure is a part of your growing process. People will fail you, and you will fail them. These events are all part of life, and it is not always personal; it's how you respond to these events and situations that make the difference.

Cast down wicked imaginations as they arise and don't allow them to fester. Get in the habit of being mindful of your thought patterns and take note of any negative thoughts as they arise and replace them with positive thoughts and affirmations immediately. Don't take ownership of what doesn't belong to you, when your mind starts racing, slow down, and give attention to what fears are singing in your mind and address them immediately. Before I wrote my first book, the fear of not being a good writer would speak to me, and I responded with, " I will never know whether I'm a good writer or not if I never write."

After writing the book, the fear of people not purchasing or supporting my book plagued my mind. I responded to those thoughts with positive thoughts like "whoever this book was written for will purchase it" I spoke to my fears and moved forward. Lingering negative thoughts will hinder and eventually stop you from making progress. You must respond quickly and make your move. Each time you notice your mind wandering to a place where discouragement, sadness, fear, anger, or negativity reside, you have the authority and power to choose to reject those negative thoughts and shift them to be more positive.

The champion inside of you requires you to thrive, and therefore you must adopt healthy thought patterns that speak to your purpose. Wake up each day with a new determination to conquer your soul wound and cast down negative thought pattern that doesn't serve you.

I CAN WIN!

I WILL WIN!

I MUST WIN!

Athena Jackson

i
can
AND
I Will

A WINNING BELIEF SYSTEM

Prayer and Scriptures

Father, in the name of Jesus,

You said in your word whatsoever a man thinketh in his heart, so is he. Therefore, I know my thoughts influence my life. I am commanding my mind to come in line with your word, so my life reflects the plans you have for me. Thank you, father, for allowing me the opportunity to walk in a new belief system. Father continues to give me the strength as I learn to cast down wicked imaginations and spirit of fear and learn to trust you more each day. Father I put my trust in you, I trust that through you, all things are possible. Give me the strength to learn from my mistakes and grow; I will no ponder on my downfalls. Lord, as I embrace this new journey to serve you in my new belief system, continue to download in my spirit your wisdom, knowledge, and understanding. In Jesus name. Amen

Ephesians 4:22-24 (ESV)- To put off your old self, which belongs to your former manner of life and is corrupt through deceitful desires, and to be renewed in the spirit of your minds, and to put on the new self, created after the likeness of God in true righteousness and holiness.

Colossians 3:10 (ESV) - And have put on the new self, which is being renewed in knowledge after the image of its creator.

Ephesians 4:1-32 (ESV) - I, therefore, a prisoner for the Lord, urge you to walk in a manner worthy of the calling to which you have been called, with all humility and gentleness, with patience, bearing with one another in love, eager to maintain the unity of the Spirit in the bond of peace. There is one body and one Spirit—just as you were called to the one hope that belongs to your call— one Lord, one faith, one baptism,

Philippians 4:8 (ESV) - Finally, brothers, whatever is true, whatever is honorable, whatever is just, whatever is pure, whatever is lovely, whatever is commendable, if there is any excellence, if there is anything worthy of praise, think about these things.

Day 2

THE POWER OF PRAYER

"Prayer is the key that unlocks all the storehouses of God's infinite grace and power. All that God is and all that God has is at the disposal of the prayer. But we must use the key. *Prayer can do anything that God can do, and as God can do anything, prayer is omnipotent.*'-Dr. Reuben Archer Torrey

Prayer is simply communing with God; he has given us access to him through Jesus Christ. It is a beautiful thing that God allows us, in our imperfect nature, to commune with him. He will enable us to bring him our concerns, our needs, our hurts, our victories, our brokenness, name It, he allows you to bring it to him in prayer.

Everyone prays differently, so don't get caught up un how to pray. I love to walk and pray; my mother would kneel and pray; my sister prays on her face. I learned to walk and pray from my babysitter, who was one of the mothers of our church; she would walk and talk to God like he was right there. Out nowhere, she would start praying. My mother would make us kneel and pray because that's how she preferred to pray, but she would also sit an pray. The church I was raised in taught us to have prayer hours 3,6,9 and 12 both am and pm. I believe this is why no matter what situation I was in, I learned to take it to God. I have my way of talking to God, I always start my prayers with, Father, in the name of Jesus, because God requires us to go through Christ to speak to him. (1st Timothy 2:5 For there is one God, and there is one mediator between God and men, the man Christ Jesus)

My order of prayer

- **Contrition**: Asking for God's forgiveness.
- **Adoration**: Praising God.
- **Petition**: Asking God for a favor.
- **Thanksgiving**: Showing God gratitude.
- Allow a few minutes for God to speak to me (Waiting)

1st Thessalonians 5:17 Encourages us to "Pray continually. " God allows us to operate in our free wills. Therefore, he is not going to beg you to communicate with him, although he loves it when we trust him enough to communicate with him in prayer. Prayer is merely exercising your faith. Prayer deepens our relationship with God bringing us closer to him; it reminds us that we are dependent on him.

Athena Jackson

God loves it when we trust him enough to take our concerns to him and lay them at the altar. He also loves it when we acknowledge our wrongdoing and asks him for forgiveness. God loves to be appreciated praised and adored; throughout his word, he tells us to praise him. Praise releases our blessings. I am reminded of the saying, "When praises go up, blessings come down. Psalms chapter 100 tells us to:

1. Make a joyful noise unto the Lord, all ye lands.

2. Serve the Lord with gladness: come before his presence with singing.

3. Know ye that the Lord he is God: it is he that hath made us, and not we; we are his people and the sheep of his pasture.

4. Enter into his gates with thanksgiving and his courts with praise: be thankful unto him and bless his name.

5. For the Lord is good; his mercy is everlasting, and his truth endureth to all generations.

Like we want to be appreciated so does god; remember we are made in his image. He doesn't want us to only come to him in our time of need, but we should also make time to thank him for his presence, grace, and mercy in our lives.

When my prayer life suffered, my anxiety would skyrocket, I would become overwhelmed from time to time. When I release my worries in prayer, God's peace takes over.

The Lord's Prayer

Matthew 6:9-15 says to then like this: "Our Father in heaven, hallowed be your name. Your kingdom come, your will be done, on earth as it is in heaven. Give us this day our daily bread, and forgive us our debts, as we also have forgiven our debtors. And lead us not into temptation but deliver us from evil."

Athena Jackson

Here are a few benefits of a good prayer life:

> **Prayer releases anxiety -** *Do not be anxious about anything, but in everything by prayer and supplication with thanksgiving let your requests be made known to God.* (Philippians 4:6) (ESV)
>
> **Prayer builds your faith -** *Therefore I tell you, whatever you ask in prayer, believe that you have received[it, and it will be yours*. (Mark 11:24) (ESV)
>
> **Prayer builds your relationship with God -** *If you abide in me, and my words abide in you, ask whatever you wish, and it will be done for you*. (John 15:7) (ESV)
>
> **Prayer allows you to confess your sins and the passageway to request forgiveness, which, in return, helps you to forgive others.** *And whenever you stand praying, forgive, if you have anything against anyone, so that your Father also who is in heaven may forgive you your trespasses.* (Mark 11:25) (ESV)

Prayer allows you to discern the will of God for your life. - *When the Spirit of truth comes, he will guide you into all the truth, for he will not speak on his authority, but whatever he hears he will speak, and he will declare to you the things that are to come. (John 16:13) (ESV)*

Prayer allows you to hear God's voice and for him to get used to hearing yours. - *Draw near to God, and he will draw near to you. Cleanse your hands, you sinners, and purify your hearts, you double-minded (James 4:8) (ESV)*

Prayer allows you to operate in the spirit of gratitude. - *Give thanks in all circumstances; for this is the will of God in Christ Jesus for you (Thessalonians 5:18) (ESV)*

Prayer allows you to operate in wisdom, and Guidance - *if any of you lacks wisdom, let him ask God, who gives generously to all without reproach, and it will be given him (James 1:15) (ESV)*

Prayer helps you set your pride aside and helps you to remain humble. - *If my people, who are called by my name, will humble themselves and pray and seek my face and turn from their wicked ways, then I will hear from heaven, and I will forgive their sin and will heal their land. (2 Chronicles 7:14) (KJV)*

Prayer is essential in our physical, emotional, spiritual healing process. - *Therefore, I say unto you, Whatsoever ye desire when ye pray, believe that ye receive them, and ye shall have them. (James 5: 15) (KJV)*

Prayer allows God to handle our enemies. - *But I say unto you which hear, love your enemies, do good to them which hate you, [28] Bless them that curse you, and pray for them which despitefully use you. (Luke 6:27-28) (KJV)*

Your prayer life is one of the most important tools and resources on your healing journey. If you struggle in this area, now is the time to work on it. It's simple, open your mouth and start talking to God, and you will begin to see

Him move in your life like never before. As you start to grow in this area, it is the enemy's job to make you doubt God; don't get discouraged to stay the course, and watch God's handy work in your life.

Athena Jackson

THE POWER OF PRAYER

Prayer and Scriptures

Father in the name of Jesus,

First, I ask you to forgive me of my sins, to create in me a clean heart, and renew in me a right spirit. Thank you for being the alpha and omega, and for being my provider, my peace, my healer, my deliverer, my protector, my Shepard, and most of all my father. I appreciate your presence in my life and for the opportunity to bring you my concerns. Lord, as I continue this healing journey, welcome you to speak to me and give me more wisdom, knowledge, and understanding. You are welcome in every area of my life. I ask you to flood out anything that is not pleasing unto you and fill me with your holy spirit. I give the holy spirit permission to lead and guide me each day, drawing me closer to you.

Thank you, God, for the work you are doing in my life, and out of gratitude, I chose to live my life as worship unto you. In Jesus name Amen.

Matthew 6:9-15 (ESV) - Pray then like this: "Our Father in heaven, hallowed be your name. Your kingdom comes, your will be done, on earth as it is in heaven. Give us this day our daily bread, and forgive us our debts, as we also have forgiven our debtors. And lead us not into temptation but deliver us from evil.

Colossians 4:2 (ESV) - Continue steadfastly in prayer, being watchful in it with thanksgiving.

Jeremiah 29:12 (ESV) - Then you will call upon me and come and pray to me, and I will hear you.

Psalm 145:18-19 (ESV) - The Lord is near to all who call on him, to all who call on him in truth. He fulfills the desire of those who fear him; he also hears their cry and saves them.

Romans 12:12(ESV) - Rejoice in hope, be patient in tribulation, be constant in prayer.

Day 3

SHAPING YOUR WORLD WITH YOUR WORDS

God created this universe with his words. In Genesis, 1:1 tells us that God merely spoke: "Let there be light, and there was light." St. John 1:1 says, " In the beginning was the word, and the word was with God, and the Word was God. A word is an Idea. God shaped this world with his ideas; you a product of his plan. Since you are made in the image of God, you, too, have the power to shape your world with your words.

Your most effective tool, weapon, and resource are your words because your words are your most powerful source. Every word you speak shapes your reality; therefore, you needed to change your belief system. Your words are a direct result of what you believe. As you learn to function from a healthy belief system, your words will change by default. You are who and what you say you are period. Matthew 17:20 tells us that "if you have faith like a grain of mustard seed, you will say to this mountain, 'Move from here to there,' and it will move, and nothing will be impossible for you."

This is why it is vital that you be rooted and grounded in God's word; the word gives you the words to speak in every situation in your life. Your health, finances, children, relationships, our loved ones, you have the power to speak over these things.

People cause more damage than they realize with the misuse of their words. Negative words hold up your blessings, damage relationships, damage self-esteem, kill dreams, a feed into generational curses. Most people do this without realizing the negative impact it's causing in their lives. I remember when I used to say, "I'm broke; I'm sick; I can't, this won't happen for me, I'm not qualified enough, People won't listen to me, etc. Little did I know I was shaping my future with these words — when my belief system changed, so made my choice of words. I chose words such as "I'm temporarily delayed of funds," "God is healing my body," and so on. I refuse to speak damnation into my own life.

Each morning I wake up to motivational resources; I spend at least 30 min downloading positivity in my spirit, all of which contain the word of God. Motivational resources help to set my tone for the day. I also take time to speak over my life by using positive affirmations each day.

Athena Jackson

When I am faced with a challenging situation, I speak to my anxiety and fears as they arise. I speak over my life daily by reciting the word of god and his promises.

There is power in the words you hear from the music, television shows, and the people you surround yourself with; they have an impact on your belief system. Take note of what your listening to because it gets into your spirit. You will find as you are healing, your choice of music may change, and the people are surrounded by my change. You will not be able to tolerate negativity and will distance yourself by default.

Exercise

Write down some of the negative words you habitually repeat. Example: I'm broke, I'm sick, my kids are bad, etc.

Rewrite those words, so they fit into your new belief system

_____

_____

_____

Athena Jackson

_____
_____
_____
_____
_____
_____
_____
_____
_____
_____
_____
_____
_____

Remember, you have within yourself the power to change, heal, and deliver any situation with the power of your words. Your words can either keep you stagnant or catapult you into you to the next level. It is all in how to you chose to use them. The words that you activate in the atmosphere have a boomerang effect go back into your spirit. So be mindful of your conversations.

SHAPING YOUR WORLD WITH YOUR WORDS

Prayer and Scriptures

Father, in the name of Jesus,

You said in your word that death and life are in the power of the tongue. As of this day, I choose to speak life. I decree and declare that no weapon formed against me shall prosper, even those created by my past words. As of this day, I choose to operate in your word, and your word will become my words. I decided to exercise my authority over the enemy with the power of the word. Father, I activate a victorious, prosperous, and successful life as a result of my new belief system and my new word choices. In Jesus name. Amen

Psalm 19:14 (ESV) -Let the words of my mouth and the meditation of my heart be acceptable in your sight, O Lord, my rock, and my redeemer.

Ephesians 4:29 (ESV)- Let no corrupting talk come out of your mouths, but only such as is good for building up, as fits the occasion, that it may give grace to those who hear.

Isaiah 55:11 (ESV)- So shall my word be that goes out from my mouth; it shall not return to me empty, but it shall accomplish that which I purpose, and shall succeed in the thing for which I sent it.

Proverbs 18:21(ESV) - Death and life are in the power of the tongue, and those who love it will eat its fruits.

Ecclesiastes 10:12(ESV) - The words of a wise man's mouth win him a favor, but the lips of a fool consume him.

BELIEVE
*In Yourself
and
You Will Be*

Unstoppable

Day 4

FAITH IS YOUR SUPERPOWER

Faith is completely trusting or having confidence in someone or something. If you want to blossom into the person you were created to be, you have to put trust your creator. Your creator knows you more than you will ever know about yourself. The reason people struggle within is because of where they put their trust. People put their trust in other's opinions of them or how they view themselves. When we trust in and see ourselves through a faulty belief system, we are bound to failure. When we put our trust in other people, we are limiting ourselves to their flawed belief system. If you want to live the life God created for you, you must put your total trust in his thoughts and plans for life.

Faith gives us the confidence to Heal on purpose. It provides us with the strength to win the battle in our minds. Our fears are conquered through faith. As you invest time in becoming close to your creator and reading his word, your faith gets stronger.

Your battles are won in your faith-based mindset. Depression, anxiety, and fear are conquered by building your faith. Faith gives you the fuel you need to overcome your past and embrace your future. Faith is how we please God. Hebrews 11:6 tells us that without faith, it is impossible to please God. Trust adopts God's belief system about who we are.

Faith allows you to overcome any self-sabotaging habits and fears that do not line up with God's purpose for your life. Faith will enable you to remain loyal to your dreams when they don't look obtainable. Faith will keep you focused on God's will for your life. Faith will make you comfortable with being uncomfortable, and you will learn to submit your daily habits and routine to God's will for your life.

Faith helps you to wait on God. Faith will help you learn NOT to your understanding, trust him, and acknowledge him in all of your ways. (Proverbs 3:5-6) When we surrender our lives to our creator and adopt the kingdom mindset that with God, all things are possible (Matthew 19:26), we become unstoppable. Faith is what makes the difference between the life of average and the life of a champion. A champion refuses to concede to the mental attacks of the enemy. He knows that he is more than a conquer because his creator told him he was. His faith in his creator has more impact than the opinions of other people.

When we align our faith with the thoughts of our creator, we gain access to our inner greatness. (1st John 4:4 Greater is he that is in us than he who is in the world.) When our faith embraces God's vision for our lives, His vision becomes our vision, and it launches us into our destiny. Faith attacks any limiting belief system that does not align with God's word and his plan for our lives. It attacks a mediocre, compromising mindset that is designed to keep us stuck.

Your faith in God and his thoughts toward you will allow you to release anything and anyone that does not serve you. You will adopt a standard that keeps you from settling for people who speak against God's thoughts toward you. You are unique and precious to God, and if people can't see you in the same manner, your faith in our creator will separate you from them.

The enemy's goal is to make you second guess God. If you think about it, he has been working from the day you were born to make you question God. He knows if he can keep you separated from God, he will have control over your destiny. When you are second-guessing your abilities and your worth, understand that the devil is working to keep you in bondage to an old unhealthy belief system.

To increase our faith, you must spend time with God. Take time each day to talk to him and read his word. Set aside time each day to be silent and hear from God. As you Heal on Purpose, Allow him to reveal you the purpose for which he created you. Get to know him so that you will have the tools you need to blossom into your best self.

Day 5

EMBRACE YOUR UNIQUENESS

All of us were born with unique genetic codes and body. We are all made up of a unique bone structure, and although we may possess similar gifts and talents, there will never another you. You are unique in every aspect of your life. You are unique in how you view the world interaction with others. You are unique in how you create your world, in how you need to be loved and handled. You are unique In your beliefs — no one else in the world who thinks like you.

People waste precious time trying to blend in and be like other people; even worst, they don't have a clear vision of where they are going or where they belong. They lack the confidence to become the person they were meant to be. Our graveyards have become populated with people who didn't dare to tap into their inner greatness. While you have breath in your body, you can gain the confidence you need to live the life you were created to live.

BELIEVE
*In Yourself
and
You Will Be*
Unstoppable

Athena Jackson

Confidence is the secret to embracing your uniqueness

- Know your purpose. It's is difficult to believe in a person you don't know; this includes yourself. You can't be confident in yourself when you don't have a clue why you were created or what your purpose is. The secret to understanding your purpose in forming a relationship with your creator and reading the manual he designed for us to have a victorious life, the bible.

- Know your potential. God gives you dreams for a reason; your dreams are an indication of what it is you were created to become. If all you do is dream about teaching, then know that you can teach. You can do whatever you want to do. The only person that can stop your show is you.

- Know your source. Everything you need, god has it. He is your source, and the more you rely on Him and not man, your faith will grow. Understand that God has equipped you with everything you need within yourself blossom. An apple seed has everything it needs to produce a tree full of apples. When God created you, He created you to succeed.

- Know your worth. Everything God created, he created to succeed in its purpose, and it has value. The just as the sun does not seek your permission to shine or birds need your permission to fly, you don't need validation and authorization to live on purpose.
- Know your uniqueness. You are an original, and there is no one else like you, embrace that fact. Don't try to be like anyone else but be comfortable in your skin. Comparing yourself to others will keep you stagnant and doubting yourself. You are you, and you are enough.

Embrace your uniqueness; it sets you apart from a world full of people trying to imitate other people. It is ok to stand out in a crowd. Trying to match yourself to your family, friends, co-workers, or the people you admire is a recipe for misery. The less you compare yourself to other people the happier you will be in life. Allow your uniqueness to help you discover more of yourself each day.

Day 6

THE MINDSET OF A CHAMPION

Life has a way of throwing blows at us; whether it's a natural catastrophe, abuse, abandonment, divorce, or tragedies, to overcome these events, we must adopt the mindset of a champion. The greatest attribute of a champion is their unwavering faith. They understand Romans 8:7 when it tells them that " Nay in all these things, we are more than conquerors through him that loves us." They wake up, eat, sleep, and work like conquerors. Champions don't bow to giants; they force their giants to bow to them; they believe in God and in their ability to carry out the assignment he has placed on their lives. Champions don't allow tragedies to shape their future, and they understand that their history does dictate their tomorrow. Champions allow battles to strengthen them and turn tragedies into purpose.

Oprah Winfrey is a prime example of a champion. Her cousins and uncle repetitively raped her, and a family friend, and after running away from home, she became pregnant at the age of 14 and lost the baby. It was after those traumatic events that Oprah excelled in high school, received a scholarship to college, and now is a billionaire. She had to make peace with her past and refuse to bow to the fears that plagued her mind. She was my motivation to let go of my push past my fears. Let's look another Champion, Franklin Roosevelt, he as paralyzed from the waist down due to polio before running for office, yet he was a four-time president of the United States.

These two champions refused to quit; instead, they allowed their pain to thrust them into a fantastic future. What did they have to lose, they already suffered what most people would have allowed to keep them from blossoming? Instead of becoming a victim, they chose to fight, and both go down in history as champions.

I, too, am a champion, I suffered sexual abuse from the age of five age till I was 16. For years I allowed my damaged emotions to rule my life. One day I woke up, I chose to heal on purpose so that I could walk in my purpose and do what God created to do. Today I walk in victory over my past trauma and have helped women and men all over this world start their healing journeys.

Adversity is the training ground for a champion. No matter how complicated life becomes, a champion will find solutions because they are solution-driven. Their faith is unwavering, and they are unstoppable. A champion understands he is made in the image of God and accepts that with God, all things are possible. They believe in their capabilities and don't make excuses.

Champions are open to constructive criticism, and they don't wear their emotions on their sleeves. Winners are disciplined, and they seek wisdom, knowledge, and understanding. They accept their mistakes without allowing their mistakes to hinder them from achieving the next level. Champions are consistent; they are not up today and down tomorrow. They are rooted and grounded in what they believe. Either they trust God, or they don't.

Champions make sacrifices and create habits that produce success. They deny their flesh of anything that doesn't line up with their dreams. Champions conquer the fear of failure and refuse to give in to distractions. Their lives are structured and organized. They exude excellence and reject mediocracy and average; they are determined to be great.

You were born a champion, and although life may have caused the champion in you to take a seat at times, it doesn't mean you don't hold the title. You have a choice to awaken the giant in you and live the life God created you for. You have the power to choose. Today I encourage you to renounce the life of mediocracy and average; you were destined to soar amongst the stars. It is your time to fly!

References

- Bourbeau, L. (2001). *Heal Your Wounds & Find Your True Self*. Les Editions E. T. C Inc. .

- Clammer, S. (2014). Understanding Your Core Pain. *Creative Selections By Shelly*.

- Emmons, R. (20085). *Thanks!: How Practicing Gratitude Can Make You.* First Houghton Mifflin Paper Pack Eddition.

- *https://www.biblegateway.com/*. (n.d.).

- *https://www.dictionary.com/browse/google*. (n.d.).

- Sigmund Koch, D. E. (1985). *A Century of Psychology As Science.* Mc-Graw - Hill.

- *The Holy Bible, English Standard Version.* (2008,2011, and 2012). Crossway. (Copeland, 1997)

- Copeland, G. (1997). *Prayers That Avail Much.* Harrison House.

I Healed on Purpose

Athena Jackson

You can't go back and change the beginning, **but you can start** *where you are and* **change the ending.**

I Healed on Purpose

CPSIA information can be obtained
at www.ICGtesting.com
Printed in the USA
LVHW040922221119
638065LV00002B/331/P